This book is dedicated to my mother, who taught me to love truth, goodness, and beauty without the help of any theories at all.

CONTENTS

Foreword

A response to our society's moral breakdown, character education is arguably the fastest growing educational reform movement in America today. A 1996 survey by the National School Boards Association found that 45% of responding school districts said they had already launched a character education initiative and another 25% said they intended to do so in the near future.

Whether this movement fades or flourishes, however, will depend in large part on whether there is good theoretical thinking to sustain and direct it. The social psychologist Kurt Lewin once said, "There is nothing so practical as a good theory." In the rush to implement character education, many school practitioners have neglected to ask basic questions: What is character? How does it develop? What virtues make it up? What is our understanding of the human person and human nature? What theories have influenced American approaches to moral and character education in the past, and what ones are at work now?

Holly Salls's book addresses basic questions like these. She brings the wisdom of a theorist and a practitioner of long experience to bear on these issues. Her work will make a much needed contribution to the national conversation about educating for character and especially to teacher formation programs.

Thomas Likona,
Author, *Smart and Good High Schools*
Cortland, New York, June 27, 2005

Preface

"That's astounding! You were interested in character education in 1974, before there was a need for it!" That comment, which astounded me more than I astounded the educator with whom I was speaking, took place in Washington DC, in February of 1995. I was attending the second annual Character Education Partnership (CEP) conference, then a newly formed group of Americans who want to promote a type of education that will help solve the increasingly serious problems faced by American youth. I was at the conference to present a paper detailing the manner in which my school teaches character.

I had been working at The Willows Academy, a private college preparatory school for girls, for seventeen years, trying initially to consolidate our efforts to found the school, and then working hard at keeping it afloat and making the initial objectives a reality. Private education is not an easy task, and educators who have chosen to work within it can attest to the amount of time and commitment it requires.

It was not until a friend convinced me to present an abstract for the CEP conference that I really ventured beyond the confines of my individual efforts. The experience of the CEP conference, however, sharpened my awareness of the importance of our work at The Willows and made such an impact on me that I could no longer be content to go about the task of character education in relative isolation. I saw not only that my reasons for promoting character education differed from those of my fellow speakers but that The Willows' character education strategy was different from that of all the other speakers at the conference. As a matter of fact, what impressed me most were the many divergent reasons for character education represented at that conference, almost as many as there were speakers. We were all educating for character, but doing so for different reasons, and many of the resultant strategies were at odds with each other.

Another conversation that took place at the Washington conference, this time with an Assistant Superintendent of a school district, was about teaching what he called "values/virtues." He was describing to me the difficulty his school district was experiencing in reaching a consensus of teachable values/virtues, since each child is an individual, and therefore unique. I, thinking along different lines, suggested that students must have something in common. If not, how could we teach them anything at all as a group? I proposed the existence of a common humanity, the possible basis of some values/virtues that all children could acquire. The Assistant Superintendent immediately lowered his voice and told me confidentially that, if what I meant by speaking of our "common humanity" was human nature, I should take care not to talk about it, as no one would take me seriously any longer. That was the final blow to my isolationist life. I needed to study this issue more closely to be able to talk about the character education carried out at The Willows in terms understandable by people of differing ideologies.

In order to write this book I did a broad bibliographical search of American and European educational journals dating from the 1980s to the present. When quoting from sources written in Spanish, I have taken the liberty of providing my own translation. I chose selected writings of John Dewey and Alasdair MacIntyre regarding character education, setting aside much of their other philosophical reflection. In addition, I cite authors who are currently writing about character education and whose insights have been invaluable in my own analysis. Some of these authors are currently involved in the American educational system, and others are outside our cultural milieu; they are all wrestling with the same dilemma, however - the best way to educate for character.

Holly Salls,
Chicago, IL
August 15, 2005

ACKNOWLEDGEMENTS

Thanks to:

Tom Lickona, for asking about this book every time we ran into each other at conferences, in airports or simply by email. Without his encouragement, this book would not have been published.

Madonna Murphy, for guiding me through the "new author" experience and for being so consistently encouraging.

Mom, for all of her last-minute typing and everything else that she did to make this book a reality.

Theresa Civantos. for the long hours she spent as my formatter, Laurie Salls for editing Part IV, and Laura Anderson, Amberly Glitz, Caitlin Glitz and Lily Civantos for their careful reading while I plowed furiously ahead.

INTRODUCTION

Contemporary educators who are themselves the products of American colleges and universities will certainly agree that teacher preparation in the United States is aimed primarily at practice and not at theory. Even though the saying goes that there is nothing more practical than a good theory, the following story illustrates why I consider this book a *risk*.

During a summer course at a local university, one of my classmates confessed that she had enrolled because she wanted to know if she really had the obligation to refrain from indicating right from wrong and good from bad in her character education classes. Her school district was using a methodology based on the study of moral dilemmas and she was expected to limit her comments regarding student responses to statements such as "that is interesting." Even though she had no formal philosophical training, she did not feel comfortable pretending to be neutral, limiting her reactions to "that would be illegal."

This young teacher realized innately that elementary and secondary educators *need* to ask themselves fundamental questions such as *What is education? What is character education? What is the role of the teacher in education? Is there a valid type of education that is not character education as well?* Only after answering these questions can one truly be an effective educator. It is only after answering these questions that teachers have a grasp of the depth of the task confronting them each day.

I have chosen three topics for close examination: an historical overview of character education in The United States, John Dewey's educational philosophy, his theories of character and its training, and Alasdair MacIntyre's moral philosophy and his conception of educating for good character. The fourth section is an elaboration of my own thought, which, I hope, will help enrich the American tradition of character education.

Part I is an introduction in which I examine a variety of issues essential to a theoretical understanding of character education itself. The first is the relation of character education to moral philosophy and a short overview of Immanuel Kant, Aristotle, and Lawrence Kohlberg. Next, for a fuller understanding of American character education, I present survey of its development since Colonial times; emphasizing the place that teaching for good character has historically held in American education.

The remainder of Part I is dedicated to a description of the most influential trends in character education since the 1960s. This, along with the historical overview, provides the reader with an idea of the character education that we have inherited from the past and the contemporary conception of character education in the United States. Placing contemporary trends within their historical context is helpful in understanding how and why educational thought has evolved in addition to identifying which future initiatives would be within the spirit of the traditions that have preceded them.

Researchers explain the amazingly rapid acceptance of Values Clarification in the 1960s by pointing to the accompanying methodologies, designed to be implemented without in-depth theoretical preparation. As we learned from that experience, those who put methodologies into practice may not be aware of the philosophical tenets behind what they teach, but each program and every trend in character education is based on a theory and all theories have desired outcomes. Every methodology stands on a specific definition of the human being, a specific understanding of what society is, and a definition of education.

Regrettably, educators are rarely offered the opportunity to think about these underlying issues. Without explaining the theoretical foundations upon which they are based, many school districts expect teachers to put methodologies into practice because of the results that they are purported to supply. As a result, teachers frequently forward theories and philosophies of which they are unaware.

Because of the importance of knowing the theory behind the practice, Part II describes not only John Dewey's ideas concerning character training and educational methodology, but more importantly, it discusses his notions of the human person, morality, society, and character education. No other philosopher has had a greater impact on American public education than Dewey. Nevertheless, without understanding his theoretical framework, teachers use practical applications of Dewey's philosophy unaware of the principles that gave rise to them and the educational consequences that those principles were designed to promote.

Although he set the stage for American character education, John Dewey's ideas do not reign uncontested. To illustrate a different philosophical tradition, Part III is devoted to the writings of Alasdair MacIntyre. He argues that the Aristotelian concept of education in virtue provides a solid base for character development, offering a philosophical tradition that defines person, education, and society from a point of view much different from Dewey's and resulting in an interesting alternative.

The choice of Dewey and MacIntyre was not merely a random sampling of American philosophical thought. I chose Dewey because of his overwhelming influence on the practice of teaching in America and I took on MacIntyre because his alternative could lead to a much needed renewal of character education in this country.

Part IV advances some of my own ideas about character education, combining aspects of Dewey's education for democracy and MacIntyre's education in virtue. My contributions to the character education debate are also based on my personal experience as a classroom teacher and as a school administrator. My adventures as a teacher, the experience of creating and running co-curricular activities programs, my efforts to structure a school-wide mentoring program, the time and energy that I have spent creating a character education program for my school and, most of all, my personal experience as a teacher of character have shaped the experiential paradigm within which my proposals have been formulated.

Education, especially character education built on textbooks, activities and methodologies that are marketed as *teacher-proof* are symptomatic of many theorists' serious misunderstanding of the essence of education. Character education is successful not because it is *teacher-proof* but rather because it is *teacher-dependent*. Teachers who are expected to educate for character must have the opportunity to reflect upon the theories that inspire the methodologies that they put into practice.

To make character education better, teachers should be encouraged to assume more than simply a functional role. Teachers should be given time to reflect on character and character education in terms of the questions suggested above. Character education can step into the future more sure of its nature and what it wants to accomplish if the personal reflection of educators, professionals who are so busy that reflection seems the antithesis of their calling, forms part of its foundation.

PART I
CHARACTER EDUCATION:
an introduction

Philosophy & Character Education

The Need for Character Education

The question of how to develop good character is not a new one. The need to teach character is schools is not new, either. The fact that we need to teach character to our children links us to Plato, Aristotle, Kant and Piaget. Teaching good character has been at the heart of educational philosophies since the times of Plato, who wondered whether virtue could be taught at all. Aristotle lamented,

> In modern times there are opposing views about the practice of education. There is not general agreement about what the young should learn either in relation to virtue or in relation to the best in life: nor is it clear whether their education ought to be directed more towards the intellect than towards the character of the soul. The problem has been complicated by what we see happening before our eyes, and it is not certain whether training should be directed at things useful in life, or at those conducive to virtue, or at nonessentials. All these answers have been given. And there is no agreement as to what, in fact, does tend toward virtue. Men do not all prize most highly the same virtue, so naturally they differ also about the proper training for it.[1]

All societies have wrestled with the problem of educating their children to be good citizens and, consequently, they have produced many theories of what constitutes good character, of educating for good character and also many moral philosophies that support their views. Plato, Aristotle. Kant and Piaget all sought the best method to foster good character in young people. This is a sign of our common heritage, which should reassure us. Just as the ancients and the philosophers of the enlightenment project searched for the best response to the demands of their worlds, we search for an education that is responsive to the contemporary world and its moral dilemmas. One of the most prominent features of character education today is that there is not one universally held theory of what character education is, nor how best to teach it. There are, in fact, quite a variety of theories. We, as did our predecessors, need to define character education for the modern world in order to formulate a way of teaching it. Our first undertaking then, should be to look at the historical precedents of some current theories to understand the foundations of contemporary thought.

The Ancient Greeks

Socrates, Plato (c.428 — 348 B.C.) and Aristotle (384 - 323 B.C.) are the founding fathers of the Western philosophical tradition. Socrates and Plato thought that knowledge of the good would necessarily result in good actions. Aristotle, Plato's student, disagreed profoundly with his teacher, and developed his own theory. This theory affirms that there is a fundamental contrast between persons as they are now and persons as they could be if they fulfilled their essential nature. Aristotle argues that ethics is the science that enables persons to understand that, in order to attain their goal or télos, they need to know how to make the transition from what they are now towards a fuller realization of their human nature. The goal of all human beings is happiness, a rational happiness that is attained by acquiring virtue. Reason instructs the person as to what the goal is and how to attain it. The moral virtues are virtues of the will and of the appetites that determine how we act, educate, and order our emotions and desires toward the good.[2]

Immanuel Kant

Immanuel Kant's (1724 - 1894) philosophy, termed *deontological*, differs greatly from classical Greek thought. Kant eliminates the concept of teleology, the notion that man has a goal (happiness) that he naturally wants to acquire, and he says that human beings should not act out of a desire for happiness, but rather that they should act only out of respect for the moral law (duty). Kant's guiding moral principle is to act in such a way that your action could be used as a universal law. Individuals discover the manner in which they ought to act by submitting each of their actions to this criterion. The Kantian source of morality is reason, but on his view reason does not make a connection between action and any kind of goal. Kant argues that true morality is "autonomous," that is, not influenced by desire, inclination or the consequences of the act. Man performs moral actions simply because reason dictates that they ought to be done. This is Kant's famous *categorical imperative*. Any motivation other than duty robs morality from the act, even if one is naturally inclined to do good or if the consequences of the act could facilitate its performance.[3] Thus, to use an everyday example, Kant would say that a morally good person is not moved to help a blind person to cross a busy intersection by feelings of pity or of empathy — he helps only because one should help the blind across the street (duty).

Jean Piaget

A third moral philosophy that underlies contemporary thought is the cognitive developmental or moral reasoning paradigm of morality. Initiated by Jean Piaget in the 1920s, it became widely accepted due to Lawrence Kohlberg's research into the stages of moral reasoning in the 1960s. Kohlberg's research became the basis of character education in the 1970s.

Like Kant, Kohlberg (1927 — 1987) asserts that rationality is the exclusive source of morality. For a moral person the thought process itself is the ultimate goal and moral standard. The content of the moral act is no longer important. In this aspect, Kohlberg differs from Kant, who said that duty is the only moral motivation, and from Aristotle, who said that a natural yearning for happiness motivates man to search for and to do the good. Kohlberg argues that the moral person has developed the cognitive capacity of moral reasoning appropriate for his current stage of moral development.[4]

Goals and Anticipated Outcomes

Each of these three traditions has given rise to a specific conception of morality and a specific type of character. For the most part, modern theories of character education have their roots in one of these three philosophies. When trying to determine the basis of character education today, Thomas Lickona suggests in *Educating for Character* using the intended goals and outcomes of each of them, pinpointing the characteristics each philosophy attributes to the morally good person. (EC, 246 – 47)

Moral Reasoning: Kant, Piaget & Kohlberg

In the moral reasoning model, (Kohlberg and Piaget), persons advance morally as they learn to internalize rules. Morality resides exclusively in this reasoning process that is fostered by group discussions among children, who are at the same stage of moral thinking and who come to a consensus regarding the nature of morality. The morality of an act differs from stage to stage, and as a result the child's moral stage determines the morality of specific acts for him.

A morally mature person has passed through the sequential stages of moral reasoning to the point that he can make autonomous moral decisions based on a moral code that he has personally composed.

In Kant's theory of moral reasoning, morality resides in the agent's knowledge of duty rather than in a stage of moral reasoning. The Kantian model of a moral person is the person who has the will to do what is a moral obligation or duty. The Kantian axiom is that one should fulfill one's duty to the point of suppressing inclinations when necessary, even if those inclinations are favorably disposed. The moral person subjects all of his acts to the following question: Would I want this action to be adopted as the universal law of conduct? Kantian theory shares the idea with Kohlberg that there is no pervasive moral goal that underlies individual acts. For Kant, each act stands alone in its singular morality, as does each moral agent. Each person in Kantian philosophy will have an individual moral code that can be transformed into a universal moral axiom. (AV, 43)

Aristotle: Teleological Ethics

In Aristotelian thought, ethics (morality applied to action) guides behavior toward a natural human goal — happiness. Moreover, Aristotle's moral theory has two parts: intellectual knowledge of the end and the positive disposition of the will toward morally good actions. Contrary to Kohlberg and to Kant, Aristotle does not think that knowledge alone constitutes morality. In Aristotle's thought, the intellect and the will work together. A person will perform good acts because he knows what is good and because he desires the good.(EC, 259)

Aristotle's moral theory also contains the notion of objective principles of moral goodness that are rooted in satisfying the needs of human nature. Individuals do not create an exclusively private idea of goodness; they discover moral precepts by becoming familiar with the needs of their human nature. All human beings share the same morality because they share the same nature.

In addition, Aristotle argues that things may appear good to man when they are not necessarily good for him. This reality requires a constant "realignment" of the will and of the appetites so that they direct themselves toward what is truly good for the person. This effort develops virtue, a stable inner disposition that makes doing what is good easy. (AV, 50) The morally good person has good habits (virtues) and knows what is good. A good person continues to strive toward goodness and happiness throughout life — he is not good simply because he does his duty or because his responses are appropriate for a person in a given stage of moral reasoning. He is good because he continually tries to do and to be good.

Foundations of Contemporary Trends in Character Education

Knowing Kant's, Kohlberg's, and Aristotle's thoughts regarding the actions that a morally good person would perform and the philosophical foundation that each man uses to determine the characteristics of a good person, we can now look at the modern trends in character education. We should be able to recognize their philosophical foundations and as a result, foresee their definitions of good character. We can also better understand adults brought up within these trends and the reason that they define *good* in a specific way.

Knowing which philosophies support what character education proposals, we can take an educated stand in favor of one or several of them. A preference for one kind of proposal over another does not imply a blind refusal to recognize valuable contributions of other thinkers. People with divergent points of view have made important contributions in the area of teaching methodology and educators of all types have gladly adopted them. Methodology can frequently be part of the "free zone" in the discussion of educational philosophy, an area in which contributions from many philosophies enrich classroom instruction.

Chapter 1
Historical Background

The modern experience of character education forms part of the history of American education, which, since its beginnings, has tried to balance the interplay between diversity and unity. Today there is not simply one American experience of education, nor is there one experience of character education. In his book *American Education: The Colonial Experience*, Lawrence Cremin writes that "diversity and with it the attendant phenomena of cultural competition, accommodation, and blending was from the very beginning a fundamental fact of American life."[1]

Education for good character was central to the European educational traditions that molded Colonial America. Each tradition brought a distinctive understanding of good character, its own ways of educating for good character, and its own ideas about who should carry out this task. As Adolphe Meyer writes in *An Educational History of the Western World*, "Although time was to snuggle them under the British wing, the colonies were peopled by a folk vastly varied."[2]

Early America

Most people think of the Puritan colonies when thinking of Colonial America. They assume that American culture derives only from these first settlers. This oversimplification makes it difficult to understand the diversity that characterizes American culture, its education and its character education. In reality, Colonial America was made up of three distinct settlements: the Puritans in New England who were Calvinists, the Southern settlers who belonged to the Church of England, and the Middle colonies, most of whom initially were from Holland and the Dutch Reformed Church. Each of the three sections of Colonial America had a specific religious spirit that would play a crucial role in the development of the character education distinctive of each community.

The Puritans, who left England to found a Calvinistic community free from the domination of the Church of England, were the most severe in their outlook on life and on good character. For them, God was demanding and children needed to be trained in self-denial, in rigorous discipline, and, above all else, in obedience to authority. The Puritans taught their children character within the family - principally by reading the Bible. This was common practice both in colonial America and in England. Because the Puritans believed in salvation through Scripture, education was very important, not only for systematically transmitting their intellectual heritage, but also for pursuing a cultural ideal. Family, church, school, the community itself all of society was dedicated to the task of molding men.

The Southern colonies were an economic investment rather than a place of religious freedom. These settlers were comfortable in the English political and religious systems. Theirs was a less intense attitude towards religion and education. They thought of God as distant, benevolent, and undemanding. They tended to be more indulgent and affectionate with their children than the Puritans. They viewed character education in terms of developing decorum, respect, and duty. Conserving a tradition that they brought from England, families wanting formal education for their children employed private tutors within the home. These tutors were supposed to inculcate the attitudes appropriate to their students' position in society. The government of the Southern colonies took little interest and few initiatives in education.[3]

Dutch commercial enterprises founded the Middle colonies of New York and New Jersey, bringing along with them the Dutch culture and the Dutch Reformed Church. The religious tolerance of the Dutch Reformed Church differentiated them from the Puritans to the north and from the Anglicans to the south. These colonists had a more moderate temperament, and they taught their children to control passion through reason, virtue, and piety.

William Penn founded Pennsylvania, the third middle colony. It was originally intended to be a "Quaker commonwealth, a holy land of virtue and good works, where gambling, swearing, and guzzling were outlawed." Since they believed that each Quaker was directly connected to God and did not need educated clergy to lead them, Quakers had little interest in primary education, and even less in higher education. Pennsylvania allowed the groups of settlers that formed their colony complete religious freedom. The Quakers also tried to accommodate each denomination's emphasis on education by granting each religious group the authority to provide its own education, houses of worship, and hospitals, three tasks typically undertaken by religious leaders of the times. As in both the Southern and the Northern colonies, primary education in Pennsylvania took place within the family, and the Bible was used as the basic reader. (EHW, 209, 10)

Using the Bible to teach reading was standard in all of Colonial America because it taught a combination of religion and Christian behavior. It is interesting to note that one of the primary goals of all colonial education was teaching good character. The churches actually played a minor role in the character education of colonial children because society expected adult members of the community to teach good character. (SSC, 5)

The Eighteenth Century

During the eighteenth century, American character education changed very little in the way that it was carried out, although its tone altered significantly. In the towns along the Atlantic coast, life was relaxed and the rigidity evident in the early days had loosened up.

In Virginia,

[Tutors] fashioned in the genteel English tradition... put their confidence in the ancient classics and needless to say, in mannerly deportment, piety and rectitude... Nor were the young ladies of quality forgotten in the gen-

eral shuffle. Like their brothers, they addressed themselves to the axioms
of the catechism and the theory and exercise of decorum. (EHW, 200)

The development of good character took on a more leisurely and moderate
pace, since social stability allowed male children to remain in the same town and
to join the family enterprise. Parents could afford to take a long-term approach
to education, unlike parents in the western frontier. These pioneering families
felt the urgency of completing a child's character development at an early age so
that he could go into the frontier. Easterners had the luxury of being able to accomplish character education in a variety of ways in the nuclear family, through
the schools and churches or with the help of neighbors. Although the basic
moral rules had not changed, occasional deviations were not seen to be overly
threatening. By the eighteenth century American families had formed strong
communities that provided an education in both good behavior and religion.
(SSC, 9-10)

The Nineteenth Century

The American Revolution of 1776, its new ideas, and the independence it
brought the young colonies set the scene for a radical transformation in American society. During the mid-eighteenth century the vast majority of American
families lived on family farms that were relatively self-sufficient. One hundred
years later, however, a significant number of families had moved away from the
small town and into the city to find jobs in manufacturing, construction, trade,
and transportation.[4] Because larger scale manufacturing was gaining the com-
petitive advantage over traditional family enterprises, children had to seek economic security away from home, and it was no longer possible to educate them
slowly. (SSC, 24)

Fathers, who in earlier times were the main moral educators, now worked
away from home. Thus the moral education of children fell to the nineteenth
century mother. This rearrangement of family circumstances provoked a transformation both in child-rearing practices and in the mother's role in the home.

The mother now became the dominant family figure, "creating with her
strength, devotion, piety, and knowledge the ambiance within which proper nurturing could proceed."(NE, 372-73) Society expected her to exemplify Christian
virtue in her own life and to inculcate virtues in her children by means of daily
readings, exhortations, and lessons in proper conduct. Mothers cultivated an
inner desire for virtuous living in their children and forged a tie between virtue
and happiness. (SSC, 24)

This new urban domesticity contributed to a marked separation between
household and community that was new to American society. Rural Americans
were accustomed to small farming communities where neighbors looked out for
each other. This distinction between household and community also made a
clear distinction as to who had the right to educate (above all, the mother) and
who needed to be counteracted. There was also a general feeling that mothers
needed to prepare children to live among people who were potentially harmful.
This preparation needed to be done quickly, as children of twelve frequently left

home in search of jobs. They needed strong and early character education before they left home so that their employers could not deceive them. Bosses were seen as self-interested corrupters of youth, as were strangers in general. A powerful conscience and a strong commitment to basic values, however, would save children from the evils of the larger society. Calvinistic emphasis on early childhood education gained renewed importance along with an early and intense character education. All of this meant that primary education needed to be structured in a way that had not been necessary before. Daily and Sunday schools now took on a greater role in helping mothers fulfill their educational task. Sunday schools offered reading and writing to working children in addition to keeping them off the streets on the Sabbath. (SSC, 18-21)

The rapid growth of the common or public school from 1780-1830 was in direct response to this growing need for early character education. The focus of the common school was almost exclusively moral. The students were mainly young children, who spent several hours and successive days in class. The primers, such as the well-known *McGuffy Readers*, taught reading and stressed virtue and religion. The primers portrayed the protagonists of American history almost as Biblical heroes. George Washington, for example, was often compared to Moses. Others were exemplars of industriousness, honesty, and intelligence. Events such as Columbus's discovery of America were depicted as being guided by divine providence, and the American Revolution as having been brought to a successful conclusion by the intervention of God. The significance of American history was equated with the divine scheme for moral government.

By the 1830s, however, the goals of character education in the public schools shifted significantly. No longer solely concerned with preparing the young for a hostile world apart from the family, schools now saw their function as promoting a common culture. Behavior received special attention within the classroom good habits were encouraged and bad habits punished. The objective was winning student acceptance of certain values, cultivating a love for virtue, and developing moral commitments that would last a lifetime.

Character education in the public schools was also a means to achieve political and economic ends; it would create diligent workers and responsible citizens, men and women of virtue. In 1829, Samuel Hall, a professor in Boston, wrote:

> We see the magic influence of our schools in the habits of industry,
> sobriety, and order which prevail in the community; in the cheerful
> obedience yielded to the laws, and in the acts of charity and benevo-
> lence, which are everyday multiplied around us. [5]

Morality was a mixture of Protestantism and the nineteenth century idea of good citizenship - love of country, love of God, duty to parents, and habits of thrift, honesty, and hard work in order to accumulate property, a sure sign of progress and the perfection of the United States.

Samuel Hall gave a series of lectures addressed to prospective teachers in which we can see this emphasis on strong character. In his exhortations for an appreciation of the importance of early education he stressed that "the effects of habits formed in early childhood will be as lasting as life. ...Let them grow up unrestrained in the passions, unintelligent and immoral, and their influence must be destructive to the peace, morals, and happiness of society." (LSK, 18-21)

The primary school teachers, always single or widowed women who did not have young children, had to meet moral criteria that were considered more important than their educational preparation. A teacher had to possess common sense and uniformity of temper. She had to have the capacity to understand and discriminate character, to be affectionate, to possess decision of character, and to have a just moral discernment. (LSK, 30) These qualifications were especially important because their primary task was to exercise a strong moral influence on their students. Hall stressed that "the cultivation of virtuous propensities [in students] is more important than even their intellectual culture…the most orderly, the most moral school will make the best progress in study. Moral motives are the best inducement to a faithful improvement over time." (30, 25)

Although America was far from Europe, the liberal philosophy of John Locke made deep inroads in American thought and in its education. The "inner-directed" man lived a life of strict self-restraint and good citizenship based on the development of a powerful conscience. Scottish common sense realism gave intellectual authority to these tendencies and in 1837 one educator stated,

> Sceptered hands, a powerful aristocracy, military force, an omnipresent police force these are the means of preserving peace and order among other nations of the earth, but here they have no place. We are necessarily self-governed, and therefore the absence of these external physical restraints must be supplied by a universal infusion of moral principles. (NE, 125)

By the middle of the nineteenth century, several waves of European immigration came to American shores, and it soon became clear that these children needed to be educated regarding the life and values of America. (SSC, 27) The immigrants included Germans, Irish, Lithuanians, Polish, and Italians, many of whom were Catholic. They brought with them a cultural and religious diversity greater than that experienced in the colonies. Because of this diversity, the emphasis on specific religious doctrine in schools would eventually give way to a basic nondenominational Christian tone. Schools attempted to use generic Christianity as a common ground for character education, trying to dissolve traditional internal divisions within Protestantism. A nondenominational Christian education also reinforced traditional Protestant values, the basis for American culture until this point. Nonsectarian education allowed for public commitment to common Christian tenets, while simultaneously allowing for private differences. Public school moral education gradually became simply reading the Bible. Over time it devolved into simply a generalized set of Christian values. Sunday schools were freed from their task of teaching the rudiments of reading and writing, and they concentrated on teaching the specific religious doctrines of their church.

The attitude of the new Catholic immigrants posed an additional dilemma for character education in public schools. Catholics felt that trying to teach morality without reference to religion would lead to religious indifference, if not to abandonment of the faith. As a result, Catholics were not comfortable with the state's autonomous role in character education. Furthermore, they did not agree with relegating Church authority to the private domain. They believed that, in reality, the nonsectarian schools were Protestant. As James Burns puts it in his book *The Principles, Origin and Establishment of the Catholic School System in the United States*, Catholics of those times considered that "the teachers were almost exclusively Protestant, the Protestant Bible was read, some of the books used were sectarian in character, and the atmosphere of the schoolroom was, generally speaking, such as to constitute a menace to the faith of Catholic children."[6]

Initially Catholics suggested a system of schooling in which "religion of every shape and form be excluded. Let not the Protestant version of scripture, Protestant forms of prayers, Protestant hymns, be forced on the children of Catholics, Jews and others as at present, in schools for the support of which their parents pay taxes as well as Presbyterians." (PO, 361) The Protestants did not accept this point of view because they held political power. Ultimately, the Catholic population preferred and established an independent system of education in which they could teach morality within the context of their faith.

Public school supporters never accepted private education and, in order to eliminate private education, many legislative battles took place over funding. In 1842, New York's legislature passed a law that denied funding to any school teaching religion. (PO, 372) Legislatures found it more and more difficult to justify Protestant Christianity in public schools, and they were forced to increase religious neutrality in public schools, thus weakening the theological content of the character education taught. (NE, 168)

Thus began the separation of character from religion in American public schools and in many people's minds. The definitive break did not come until 1963, when non-denominational prayer in public school was declared unconstitutional, violating the separation of Church and State.

1890s - 1940s: Effects of Modernity

From 1890 - 1940 a great social change took place because of the rapid industrialization and urbanization of American society. Until then the divergent aspects of life had been united in the highly personal context of neighborhoods and communities. Faced with the need to find employment outside this unifying environment, individuals began to lead increasingly divided lives - work, leisure, home, and church, each had different rules that rewarded different values. (SSC, 47) Now success depended not so much on character as on skill, efficiency, and social competence. Technical advances required schools to expand their function and to teach social, academic, and vocational skills so that students could succeed in a variety of roles. Because of these marked changes in the American lifestyle, educators began to doubt the adequacy of traditional forms of character education.

From 1900 - 1940 educators responded in two major ways to modernization and urbanization: they founded the Character Education Movement, which sought to teach specific virtues and traits of good character, and also the Progressive Movement, which emphasized a flexible and critical approach to character education without any specific moral tenets. It sought to create a character education that would meet the needs of an ever-changing social order. (SSC, 36-7)

The Character Education Movement was more programmatic than theoretical. It firmly believed that the modern world and traditional values were compatible as long as children were taught correctly. Between 1900 and 1920 their programs grew slowly, but by 1925 their emphasis on moral codes became the distinguishing factor between the Character Education Movement and the Progressive Movement. The Character Education Movement was strongly influenced by some new youth organizations: Boy Scouts, Campfire Girls, and the 4-H Clubs. These new youth groups emphasized elaborate codes of conduct and used group processes to foster good behavior. The Character Education Movement also used moral codes to provide specific themes for character education, trying to make all aspects of school life positive moral experiences.

This emphasis on group interaction set the Character Education Movement apart from the nineteenth century style of character education and satisfied a need of the new social order - cooperation. Schools using these codes gave students citizenship grades and individual counseling. Good character was having the resolve to do the right thing, and character education was now a matter of motivation rather than ethical thinking. The moral codes encouraged by the youth groups and the Character Education Movement gave students a way to understand the connection between individual conduct and the public good, but they did not root character education in any ethical system. (SSC, 54) The Character Education Movement began to decline in the 1920s, when Hartshorne and May published research throwing the effectiveness of didactic moral education into question. Later research, however, demonstrated that the findings of Hartshorne and May were not entirely accurate, but since that time supporters of didactic character education have had to do battle against the perception that theirs is an old-fashioned and therefore inadequate response to the demands of modern society.

In contrast to the Character Education Movement, the Progressive Movement was based on the idea that one must abandon the outmoded practices and theories of traditionally taught character education. The character education advocated by the Progressive Movement aimed at efficiency. It was critical of programs that emphasized codes and specific virtues. The Progressive Movement advocated the creating a just society based on science, reason and an ethical flexibility that embraced relativity of values. Relativity, they proclaimed, was the result of the permanently fragmented nature of American life: every segment had its own moral code, many times differing from each other in what they considered appropriate ethical behavior. Situations now determined the nature of ethical behavior, and students were taught appropriate reactions to life, rather than universally applicable criteria.

With the acceptance of Progressivism, character education focused on great social and political issues rather than concentrating on personal conduct. Progressivism placed more emphasis on intellect in moral education than did the

Character Education Movement, since its purpose was to foster thoughtful and effective action in the cause of social improvement. Education and specifically character education, was thought more than ever to be key in fostering democratic society both in America and abroad. (SSC, 55 - 60)

1945 to the Present

The Second World War and the Cold War that followed it afforded American schools a great opportunity to encourage character education. Educators and theorists took advantage to offer a great variety of activities designed for moral and civic growth. These activities were promoted to encourage children to see the connection between their individual characters and their civic responsibilities, their personal efforts and the national destiny. As Edwin Wynne and Kevin Ryan explain in their book, *Reclaiming our Schools*, in the 1940s and 1950s the classroom was expected to play a role in the national battle against authoritarianism and evil. The entire country was united against international perils and, as a result, subordinated all differences in character education to that cause. The result was an eclectic approach to teaching good character.[7]

As the position of the United States became more prominent in international politics, educational priorities shifted once again. The emphasis was now on the cognitive aspects of education, and there was a subtle neglect of character. Four main developments were important in this decline. First, this country needed high-level technological and scientific skills. Schools now began to emphasize preparation for college education. Second, the pervasive anti-communism in society took attention away from other topics that had historically been subjects of character education. Third, there was now a sharp distinction drawn between the private and public realms. Since morals were increasingly viewed as a personal matter, accepting the split between the private and public realms allowed schools to avoid religion and morals altogether. Character and morality were the private responsibility of home and church. The fourth development in education came in child psychology. New psychological theories held that children's characters were shaped within the first six years of life. This theory reinforced the trend of making moral issues a matter of private preference, relieving the schools of their responsibility in this area. (SSC, 79-82)

In the 1960s and 1970s, character education ran into very difficult times. Americans were beginning to lose faith in their ability to find common ground, because of, among other things, the Vietnam War, and difficulties in ending racial discrimination. Society was ready to overlook differences and to encourage tolerance in an effort to preserve the tenuous social peace achieved after urban riots and anti-war demonstrations. The primary social value that emerged was cultural relativism. (SSC, 82-3)

The federal government now began to assume a larger role in local education, as schooling was fast becoming the focal point for gaining new civil rights. On many occasions local schools became defensive in defiance of what they felt to be the intrusion by the federal government in affairs of local communities. In addition, litigation began to increase, thus broadening children's rights. The combination of increased litigation and broadened children's rights proved fatal to character education. Teachers modified codes of conduct in their classes that in other times had been powerful tools in character education. They adopted only those rules that assured essential school order. (SSC, 84-5)

There are two court cases in particular that played a decisive role in configuring character education: one was the Engle versus Vitale Supreme Court case of 1962, which ruled that nondenominational prayer at the beginning of class was unconstitutional in public schools; and the other was the Schemp case of 1963, in which the Supreme Court ruled that devotional Bible reading was prohibited in public schools. These decisions widened the separation of church and state, effectively putting a stop to even nondenominational values education. By the middle of the 1960s, schools had backed away from character education almost completely; having lost the social approval that previously supported it. (SSC, 85)

Chapter 2
Current Trends

The hallmark Supreme Court cases mentioned in the last chapter defini-
tively eliminated religious influence from public schools. As we shall see, now
contemporary character education frequently turns to psychology for orientation
rather than to religion.

Values Clarification

Values Clarification first gained acceptance in the mid-1960s.[1] The 1960s'
social transition caused rapid changes in American society, one of which was
children's growing inability to develop feelings of authenticity and commitment.
Educators and laymen alike thought that the learning and behavioral problems of
the classroom were one manifestation of the difficulty that children were experiencing when trying to develop values in the modern world. This was a moment
in which "children needed to learn a process of choosing values that would provide them with a sense of purpose in a world perplexingly full of options."
(SSC, 88)

The Values Clarification curriculum made a clear break with tradition in
methodology and in theory. Its goal was to help students to live in a world where
one set of values could not hold true for all people, all times, and all places.
Children needed to learn not one specific set of values, but rather the process of
valuing, which would help them develop a sense of direction and also a relationship to society that would be "positive, purposeful, enthusiastic and proud."
(SSC, 88) Because they emphasized process, Raths and Simon, the originators
of Values Clarification, avoided what they considered to be indoctrination (EC,
389) and offered a values-neutral curriculum centered on the process of choosing freely from among a series of alternative values. (RV, 56) The working assumption of Values Clarification was that children have the capacity to develop
character on their own as long as they are allowed to do so in a non-judgmental
environment that is free from adult influence in value positing. Children's na-
tures are inherently good, and because of this, they do not need any specific
value system before making choices. Their inherent goodness empowers children to make their own decisions, whatever those decisions may be.[2] When using the Values Clarification value sheets, thought sheets, weekly reaction sheets,
and action projects, students answered questions such as: "What do I value in
life?" "What do I believe in?" "What things am I interested in?" What are my
problems?" These strategies, combined with the answers that students provided,
allowed students to clarify their feelings, interests and needs. This was supposed
to enable them to develop into "confident, responsible, and optimistic people

able to have meaningful relations with society."[3] The teacher's role changed dramatically from the more traditional role teachers had assumed in the past. No longer seen as a guide and authoritative source of wisdom, teachers' roles were limited to technical ones. They used morally neutral methods, allowing children to discover moral truths through their natural interaction with other children. Teachers also used non-judgmental methods similar to the empathetic, trusting, accepting, non-judgmental and non-moralizing therapist in Rogerian non-directive therapy. The atmosphere of the Values Clarification class was "permissive and stimulating but not insistent." (ROS, 120) Because it was easy to implement, Values Clarification had an immediate appeal for teachers. With its abundance of instructional materials and pedagogical advice, Values Clarification gave teachers a sense of competence. In his book *The Rehabilitation of Virtue, Foundations of Moral Education*, Robert Sandin, points out:

> Values Clarification did not ask teachers to have "independent and advanced knowledge of the substantive issues of moral decision in order to guide students in their own explorations. It was enough if the teachers understood the stages in the Values Clarification process and were skilled in helping the student to face up to certain types of decisions."(RV, 58)

The Values Clarification program assumed that the modern teacher:

> has become aware of the indecisiveness and non-finality of his own value judgments and welcomes a model of teaching that allows him to address the issues of moral decision out of his own inadequacy. The teacher's task was to create an environment in which the students, if they so desired, could find their own values. (RV, 58)

Although Values Clarification gained immediate popularity, criticism was quick to follow, especially from parents who were wary of the moral relativism that it fostered. Values Clarification seemed to confuse principles and preferences, leaving students with the feeling that all moral positions were equally valid. According to McClellen, students could complete the Values Clarification program without learning to deal with moral conflict or establishing moral priorities; they often seemed unable to make moral decisions. (SSC, 90) In addition, Values Clarification seemed to underestimate the influence of peer pressure. Peer relations are impossible to eradicate, and even though the teacher may no longer be an authority figure in the classroom, any decision of value alternatives in a classroom is a social process. Values Clarification ran the serious risk of "coming down to the substitution of adolescent conformism for adult indoctrination as the decisive factor in the formation of values." (RV, 58)

Another serious criticism of Values Clarification focused on its claim to be value-free. In addition to favoring free choice over yielding to peer or adult pressure, rationality, justice, freedom, equality, and certain types of social values, there were serious possibilities of invasion of students' privacy plus emotional manipulation due to the types of questions asked. (SCC, 90)

Although Values Clarification is no longer the most influential model of character education, it has had a profound effect on American society. For one thing, it established the primacy of the individual over all other considerations in value positing. Because this idea is so important, it would be a mistake to dismiss Values Clarification as simply another passing fad. One cannot forget that the students who learned Values Clarification in the 1960s and 70s are now parents teaching values to their own children.

As if to support the negative influence of Values Clarification, Charles Sykes describes the mentality of typical of high school students in his book *Dumbing Down Our Kids*:

> They will not admit that something is correct, incorrect, right or wrong — they say that it is a matter of opinion. "The concept that there might be universal and objective moral principles at stake is completely alien to these youngsters... One of the striking things about spending time with high school students is the near universality of their notion that values are something they work out on their own. (DD, 164)

Given the educational background of their parents, the fact that today's teens think that the only kind of legitimate morality is private and subjective seems quite natural. Moral relativism has become as much a part of the fabric of American society as has the Protestant work ethic. "Baby Boomers" educated in Values Clarification almost universally recognize their personal and individual responsibility to create a value system. The boomers seem determined to spare their children the emotional and psychological privations they imagined that they might have suffered in their own youth. While the Depression generation made sure that the boomers would never lack material possessions, today's parents seem anxious to spare their children the stress, anxiety, and pressures of their youth. Neither of the two older generations seems to have foreseen the negative impact that such indulgence would have on younger generations deprived not only of the hardships that their parents endured, but also of the opportunities to test themselves against those challenges. (DD, 21)

Character education has repercussions that reach well beyond the walls of our schools; a child's character, whatever its qualities, determines how he or she will live as an adult. We can see once again the importance of reflection before implementing any character education programs.

Lawrence Kohlberg and the Cognitive Approach

Lawrence Kohlberg's developmental approach to character education, termed *moral reasoning*, succeeded Values Clarification, making its initial impact in the early 1970s. Although Values Clarification and moral reasoning were researched simultaneously, Kohlberg's stage theory of moral development did not appear in educational circles until Values Clarification had run its course.

Lawrence Kohlberg, a Harvard psychologist, received his Ph.D. from the University of Chicago in 1958. As part of his research, he explored the response of young men to specific moral dilemmas and by the mid-1960s he had developed a comprehensive theory of cognitive moral development. He drew heavily on Jean Piaget's research in cognitive development to formulate his own parallel theory of moral development. In *The Philosophy of Moral Development, Moral Stages and the Idea of Justice*, Kohlberg writes:

> My own work on morality started from Piaget's notion of stages and Piaget's notion that the child was a philosopher. Inspired by Jean Piaget's (1948) pioneering effort to apply a structural approach to moral development, I have gradually elaborated over the years a typological scheme describing general stages of moral thought that can be defined independently of the specific content of particular moral decisions or actions.[4]

Both Piaget and Kohlberg wanted to explain children's capacity to resolve particular types of problems: empirical analytical problems in the case of Piaget, and moral problems in the case of Kohlberg. Kohlberg's primary goal was to understand the basic concepts and reasoning involved in moral judgments and the process by which these judgments changed as children matured. Kohlberg, like Piaget, underscored the importance of social cooperation in stimulating development.

In the 1970s Kohlberg became involved in implementing educational reform by working in prisons and in schools with problem students. By the end of the decade he realized that his original theory had not provided an adequate framework for moral education in schools. To provide a more a satisfactory structure for character education in schools, he developed the concept of the "just school community," which helped stimulate students' moral development through the school's culture and its climate. Although the schools that utilized "just community" theory remedied the limitations of Kohlberg's earlier moral stage theory, this theory never had the widespread impact of his first theory. By the end of his life Kohlberg had discarded his initial theory, but the theory of moral stages had already been implemented in a great number of schools, and it is now widely held to be his most important contribution to educational thought.

The Stage Theory

Kohlberg's stage theory holds that moral development happens in six stages, and each stage has two levels. Children move through these stages in an orderly way as they develop their capacity of moral reasoning. Each stage involves qualitative differences in the manner of confronting and resolving moral problems; problem resolution is determined by the reasoning processes specific to each developmental stage. The stages range from stage one, a primitive, selfish orientation, to stage six, the fullness of moral maturity.

In stage six persons are capable of postulating the universal principles of justice, equal rights, respect for the dignity of other persons and reciprocity. These principles are autonomous, abstract, and universally applicable, independent of the specific content of the acts performed and of the cultural milieu in which the individual lives. Kohlberg writes:

This stage assumes guidance by universal ethical principles that all humanity should follow... Principles are universal principles of justice: the equality of human rights and respect for the dignity of human beings as individuals... The reason for doing right is that, as a rational person, one has seen the validity of principles and has become committed to them. (PMD, 412)

Kohlberg describes the morally mature person at Stage Six:

People have disentangled judgments about human life from status (Stage One); from its use to others (Stage Two); from interpersonal affection (Stage Three); and so on; they have a means of moral judgment that is universal and impersonal. Stage Six people answer in moral words such as duty or morally right and use them in a way implying universality, ideals, and impersonality. (PMD, 24)

It is important to note that Kohlberg describes moral development without reference to any morally specific content. The only motivation in a moral action, he argues, is the decision made by the autonomous conscience to act justly. Kohlberg left the necessity of any connection between moral knowledge and good behavior unresolved. He did admit that one can reason in terms of principles and not live up to those principles. After his work in prisons and with problem students he wrote,

I realize now that the psychologist's abstraction of moral cognition from moral action, and the abstraction of structure in moral cognition and judgment from content are necessary abstractions for certain psychological research purposes. It is not a sufficient guide to the moral educator who deals with moral concrete in a school world in which value content as well as reasoning must be dealt with. In this context, the educator must be a socializer teaching value content and behavior, not only a Socratic or Rogerian process-facilitator of development.[5]

To determine moral development, Kohlberg expanded on the dilemma method of resolving moral predicaments that Kant first introduced and that Kohlberg later expanded. Since each child is a small moral philosopher needing to discover her or his own values, teachers cannot impose their own moral decisions on children when they use the moral dilemma method to promote moral reasoning. Each dilemma can be resolved a variety of ways, therefore students must decide which solution is the best one and defend their position. The teacher's role is to initiate the moral reasoning process. They gauge student progress by the quality of their moral reasoning, not by solutions that they offer.

Kohlberg's most famous dilemmas include the dilemma in which the students must decide which person to throw out of their sinking boat in order to save the rest and the dilemma of a poor man who does not have enough money to buy expensive medication for his wife and considers stealing it. Theoretically, according to Kohlberg, any solution is a moral one if defended in a manner appropriate to the stage of moral reasoning appropriate for the student's age.

To provoke progression in moral reasoning, the dilemmas used are situations that are "hard" ethical decisions. The way to stimulate stage growth is to pose real or hypothetical dilemmas to students in such a way as to arouse disagreement and uncertainty as to what is right. The teacher's primary role is to present such dilemmas and to ask Socratic questions that arouse student reasoning and focus student listening to one another's reasons.

When using dilemmas with younger children, cases typically involve problematic situations that students can understand and with which they can identify. For example, in one dilemma, the students must decide whether, when a store security guard questions her, the main character should lie for a friend so that she will not get caught after shoplifting. (PMD, 27) In the discussion that follows, the teacher is allowed to ask clarifying questions to provoke higher level moral reasoning, but she is not allowed to encourage a specific moral response to the dilemma. From this very brief discussion we can see the way in which the Kantian concept of morality as a purely rational phenomenon has effectively been brought down to the primary and secondary school level.

The quick and widespread acceptance of the dilemma approach to character education may have been due to a combination of historical and sociological factors. Seen historically, moral reasoning is an alternative to Values Clarification, in which feeling right was more important than thinking right. When educational trends moved away from feelings, concerned educators and psychologists, Kohlberg among them, made their research public because it demonstrated that good character ought to be the result of reasoned responses to life. Kohlberg argues, "The developmental approach, first elaborated by Blatt, is one any thoughtful classroom teacher may practice. Unlike values clarification, its assumptions are not relativistic, but, rather, are based on universal goals and principles."[6]

In clear contrast to Kohlberg, whose research demonstrated that moral reasoning does develop over time, Values Clarification was not designed to promote moral development. Thus, Kohlberg's cognitive approach, designed to foster and increase moral maturity, had a growing appeal in the early 1970s.

The moral reasoning approach was an attractive alternative to Values Education because it gave educators a structure within which children could develop. It provided an alternative to the relativistic evaluation of right and wrong and it was in keeping with the pluralism that, by 1968, was a powerful social reality. The fact that any well-reasoned solution to the dilemmas was acceptable permitted educators and school districts to encourage moral growth without restricting the content of moral decisions. This is a basic requirement of American pluralism, in which all opinions have equal value and are given equal consideration and respect. Thus schools could legitimately claim to be addressing the task of helping students make moral decisions without denying their right to think as they thought best.[7]

Even after the implementation of the moral reasoning method, however, a disturbing growth in teen violence, pregnancy, and drug abuse continued: three areas that traditionally fall under the domain of character education. The focus of character education in the years between 1960 and 1990, aimed at affective and then rational moral decision making, did not bring about positive changes in American society. Edwin Delattre and William Russell write in the Boston University *Journal of Education*:

> Throughout our society we witness the lamentable results of a decades-old erosion, in both public and private life, of clarity and confidence about what it means to live our own lives with genuine integrity and to help children develop the habits of good character necessary for genuine integrity. These results hardly have to be listed; we read and hear about them daily: increased random and planned violence; gangs; drugs; rising out-of-wedlock birthrates and neglect of the young; disrespect and even contempt for so-called "traditional" families; widespread decline of academic achievement among the young. Whatever the limits and inadequacies of standardized educational tests, the fact remains that SAT scores have declined during a period of increasing funding for education and decreasing emphasis of rigorous study of subject matter.[8]

As the students of Values Clarification and moral reasoning grew older, one thing gradually became alarmingly clear: neither approach to building good character was having a lasting impact on behavior. Directly or indirectly, one would rightfully have expected a decrease in the intensity and occurrence of teenage problems. Students were capable of identifying their values and of making logical arguments as regards moral dilemmas, but somehow there was no consistent correlation between those skills and personal conduct. Although these approaches may not have lessened some social problems, they did have an impact on the approaches to parenting chosen by adults who were school children between the 1960s and the 1990s.

Self Esteem

The new approach to character education adopted by parents and schools in the 1990s was labeled the *self esteem movement*. American educators and guidance counselors decided that self esteem was the source of personality and intellectual growth, and the solution to almost every problem. When children had problems, it was the result of low self esteem, and the solution was to find ways to encourage students to think well of themselves. (GE, 69, 71)

In *Dumbing Down Our Kids*, Charles Sykes quotes the California Task Force to Promote Self Esteem as saying, "A good self-concept inoculates us against the lures of crime, violence, substance abuse, teen pregnancy, child abuse, chronic welfare dependence, and educational failure."(DD, 49) The central message of the self-esteem movement is that you are fine just the way you are. "Self love is the first source of one's personal fulfillment, happiness, and positive feelings about others." (GE, 69) Stated simply, by growing in self-esteem, children respect, cherish, and love others because they have learned to love and respect themselves.

The self-esteem movement differs from previous approaches to character education in significant ways. Values Clarification and moral reasoning were in some way supplementary to academic education, an added dimension of the educational process. The self-esteem movement links good character with academic and social success. This insertion of character education into the educational process rather than seeing it as a separate task to be done outside the academic framework is a good step; it acknowledges the positive or negative influence of children's character in all aspects of their lives.

The problem of the self-esteem approach seems to be the conceptual paradigm of the movement itself. There has been much criticism of the inward focus cultivated by self-esteem curricula, which concentrates on the child's feelings and needs coupled with constant praise. This often takes the form of stickers for young children that proclaim "I'm Terrific!" Combined with reinforcement by the teacher in the classroom, the self-esteem movement fosters the idea that everyone is wonderful just because they are who and how they are.

In addition, parents and teachers have developed what William Damon, Christina Hoff Sommers and Sally Satel call "the myth of the fragile child." In their book *One Nation Under Therapy*, Sommers and Satel write about current trends to help children develop good self-esteem.

> In 2001, the Girl Scouts of American introduced a "Stress Less Badge" for girls aged eight to eleven. It featured an embroidered hammock suspended from two green trees. According to the Junior Girl Scout Badge Book, girls earn the award by practicing "focused breathing," creating a personal "stress less kit," or keeping a "feelings diary" … Anxiety over the mental equanimity of American children is at an all-time high. In May of 2002, the principal of Franklin Elementary School in Santa Monica, California, sent a newsletter to parents informing them that children could no longer play tag during the lunch recess. As she explained, 'the running part of this activity is healthy and encouraged; however, in this game, there is a "victim" or "It", which creates a self-esteem issue.[9]

Our culture, which places such a high value on success and self esteem, has discovered that the combination of the two can only take place in an environment in which children are not allowed to suffer. In May 2003 *Psychological Science in the Public Interest* published an article that found no significant link between high self-esteem and academic achievement, interpersonal relationships, or healthy lifestyles. It did find, however, that narcissistic people and those with an inflated sense of popularity and likeability had feelings of high self-worth.

William Damon, author of *Greater Expectations, Overcoming the Culture of Indulgence in America's Homes and Schools*, says that in the self esteem movement "any attempt to link feeling good about oneself to achievement is considered both counterproductive and potentially damaging to the child's psyche."(69) Damon calls this a white lie, harmful to children's perception of self. What happens when a child receives a pleasantly meaningless message to the effect that the child is the greatest in every possible way? Damon argues that a variety of reactions can take place, each one having ramifications far beyond the child's early education. He argues that later on, especially during adolescence, when personal responsibility for one's actions assumes great importance, some children raised thinking that they are fine just the way they are cannot cope with the reality of failure and less-than-perfect outcomes. Some children simply ignore empty praise, according to Damon. Other children develop "an exaggerated though empty and ultimately fragile sense of their own powers. Still others become skeptical and reject positive feedback of any kind. Shading the truth, he insists, can easily result in undermining confidence in the message giver." (73)

When combined with American education's historical trend toward child-centeredness, the self-esteem movement can easily cause an imbalance in a child's perception of self and of the world.

> When we tell children that their first goal should be self-love, we are suggesting to them that they are at the center of the universe...This emphasis can push a child towards a narcissistic insensitivity to the needs of others. ... There is no other standard than self, and within self nothing higher than feelings. The child who completes twelve years of courses on self-esteem may or may not have a healthy self concept, but it seems possible that they will also be self satisfied egotists. (GE, 73)

The greatest weakness of the self-esteem movement is that it "draws the child's attention away from fundamental social realities to which the child must adapt for proper character development." (DD, 51)The reality of the child's obligations to family, to community is given only secondary importance. (GE, 78) Children do not learn to value guidance and feedback, but rather act as their own moral "self-referents." (DD, 53) The focus of self-esteem curricula emphasizes "needs but not obligations, feelings but not thoughts, self-gratification not self-sacrifice, self-indulgence not restraint, self-satisfaction rather than self-knowledge." (GE, 78)

Although the self-esteem movement does not seem to be a better answer to the issue of a proper character education, the shift from the external imposition of demands upon children to recognizing their internal sensibilities has had some good consequences. Adults, especially educators, psychologists, and guidance counselors, have acquired an increased sensitivity to how children think, which has led to increased adult-child communication. It seems, however, that character education theory has once again swung from one extreme to the other, from reason to feelings, without considering possible long-term effects on children educated according to these theories. (GE, 95 – 122)

Process and Content Combined

There are some educators who, recognizing previous failures to make the connection between knowledge and behavior, have put their efforts behind styles of character education that center on virtue acquisition within the "moral community" cultivated in the classroom and school. The contributions of Kevin Ryan and Thomas Lickona are an excellent and realistic step to defining the best character education for American children. Their approaches could be labeled "process and content combined," since Lickona follows in the moral stage tradition of Kohlberg, and Ryan focuses on specific content in character education, strongly appreciative of the Character Education movement of the 1920s.

Ryan writes about the importance of creating a "moral environment" within schools. Teachers and principals who make and enforce rules, give, correct, and return challenging homework assignments to students, and expect students to respect both adults and their peers sustain this kind of environment. They, as did the members of the Character Education Movement, advocate that special attention be given to mottoes, posters, pictures, pledges, symbols, songs, rituals and school ceremonies. (ROS, 178, 203-206)

Lickona develops his theory of character education around the acquisition of two virtues fundamental to a democratic and pluralistic society: respect and responsibility. He thus offers an avenue to teach character in public schools that will enhance democracy.

> Just as the value of respect is involved in the smallest everyday interactions, it also underlies the major organizing principles of a democracy. It's respect for persons that leads people to create constitutions that require the government to protect, not violate, the rights of the governed. The first moral mission of our schools is to teach this fundamental value of respect for self, others, and the environment... Responsibility is an extension of respect ... It means orienting towards others; ... Responsibility emphasizes our positive obligations to care for each other. (EFC, 44)

Lickona, echoing Kohlberg, utilizes moral dilemmas in developing moral thinking. Lickona offers concrete suggestions such as viewing discipline as "moral discipline," creating a democratic classroom, using cooperative learning, and specific guidance in the technique of moral dilemmas, all designed to help create a democratic spirit within schools. (EFC, 44, 242)

Ryan coincides with Lickona in much of his thinking, but breaks with him in the areas of creating a democratic classroom, the use of cooperative learning and the use of moral dilemmas. He advocates renewing some of the traditions that fostered character in schools earlier in our history. (ROS, 33) Both have the common goal of educating students who will be good, healthy, contributing adult members of a democratic society. For this reason they focus on virtues that foster democratic behavior. (140 - 41) Lickona's goals are the maintenance and betterment of the democratic system, while Ryan is interested in not only strengthening the democratic structure of society but also in encouraging educators to view the American educational process as part of our Western heritage.

However, the question remains of what underlying principles American educators should use in devising character education specifically for American students. Focusing the discussion of character education on virtue in the service of democratic society does not penetrate deeply enough into the philosophical foundations needed to support the best character education possible.

Should we educate our children in function of their role in a democracy, even one as cherished as the United States? Should democratic citizenship constitute the highest ideal that we offer our children? Surely we do want them to be contributing members of American society, but do we not consider our children more than properly functioning citizens? In their Boston University *Journal of Education* Edwin J. Delattre and William E. Russell write:

> Wise parents want many things for their children, but three stand out: that they should outlive their parents, that they should have salutary opportunities for happiness, and that they should deserve to be happy. They want their children to mature into morally serious people, not humorless, whose passion to do their best is not thwarted by the fact that all of us fail sometimes and that all of us die. Such parents help their children to form good habits of feeling, thought, and action early in life. They expect that doing so will lead their children toward later reflection about the nature of a life well-lived. They hope their children will come to live a good life — a life morally worth living — no matter which manifestations of honorable success, sources of deserved happiness, and adversity and disappointment it may contain.[10]

Education is first the growth of the child as a person, not primarily the education of the child in function of future participatory potential in American democracy. In fact, it can be argued that when both school and parents view education as primarily the moral growth of our youth as persons, the likelihood of successful democratic participation is increased. When understood in this way, the primary aim of education is the personal growth of each child, a growth that takes place within the context of schools that both foster an appreciation for the American democratic lifestyle and make personal commitment to American democracy possible for each child.

The Whole Child Approach

There is another line of thought in character education specifically directed toward this development of the child as a person. William Damon describes it as "constructing the whole child." (GE, 152) The whole child approach takes a middle of the road approach to its feelings-orientated and reason-orientated predecessors. Of the three approaches to educating for character discussed in Chapter 1, it most closely resembles the teleological approach, with a dose of modernization. The whole child approach to character education insists upon education of the emotions, of the intellect and of the will. These three aspects of the student's nature are educated together, reflecting the oneness of the child. The whole child orientation emphasizes virtue as well as values, rational thinking and decision- making, autonomous thought as well as the ability to utilize the advice and opinions of authorities. One interesting feature of this approach is that it does not bring with it a separate curriculum or a specific pedagogical methodology. Once an educator understands its principles, they can be applied in a flexible manner within a wide variety of educational situations.

The Ethic of Caring

The discussion of current trends in character education would not be complete without a brief discussion of the work of Carol Gilligan, a former student of Lawrence Kohlberg's, whose research regarding the development of moral reasoning specific to women has broadened character educators' vision, even though it has not yet been applied directly to the classroom. Dr. Gilligan is a professor at the Harvard Graduate School of Education, and she published her first book, *In A Different Voice,* in 1982. *In A Different Voice* deals with the moral development of women and girls: "I reframe women's psychological development as centering on a struggle for connection rather than speaking about women...as having a problem in achieving separation."[11]

With the publication of *In A Different Voice,* Gilligan led the feminist critique of Kohlberg's work, alleging a male bias in his theory of the stages of moral development. She says, "my questions are about psychological processes and theory, particularly theories in which men's experience stands for all of human experience — theories which eclipse the lives of women and shut out women's voices." (IDV, xv)

One of the conclusions drawn by Kohlberg and contested by Gilligan is that women are less capable of moral reasoning than men. Kohlberg's account of moral development focuses on rationally based moral principles, in which autonomy characterizes a high degree of moral development. In Kohlberg's stage theory, women predominantly reach the third level of moral development, that of interpersonal agreement, whereas the median level of moral development for men is the fourth level, that of law and order. (IDV, xiii) Gilligan argues that this not a valid account of women's moral development. Her research points to two distinct ethics of understanding the self and others: the male ethic, one of rights and justice, and the female ethic, one of caring and responsibility. The female ethic is contextual, rooted in concrete responsibilities of particular individuals and an understanding of self based on interdependence, affection and care of others. She states, "What for men was a process of separation, for women was a process of dissociation that required the creation of an inner division or psychic split." Gilligan's view is that, apart from emotion and interpersonal relationships, no one can analyze knowing. She points out "within the context of US society, the values of separation, independence, and autonomy are so historically grounded, so reinforced by waves of immigration, and so deeply rooted in the natural rights tradition that they are often taken as facts." When Gilligan voiced her ideas, she caused a revolution. She found that "women's approaches to conflict were often deeply instructive because of the constant eye to maintaining relational order and connection. It was concern about relationship that made women's voices sound 'different' within a world that was preoccupied with separation and obsessed with creating and maintaining boundaries between people..."(IDV, xiv)

The result of Gilligan's research is a three-stage ethic of caring that applies to women. At the first level, in which self is the only object of caring, survival is the primary goal. At the second level, in which the self seeks social acceptance, moral judgments are based on shared norms and expectations, goodness is defined as self-sacrifice, and the individual is able to protect and care for others. The third level of caring is defined by its morality of non-violence, which translates into a universal responsibility to be caring and to avoid harm.

Gilligan's ethic of caring has not had a direct impact on classroom character education, but her research has underscored the need of further consideration of the possible advantage of female-oriented character education, so that we educate girls in a psychologically more appropriate manner. Gilligan herself has pointed out that the dilemma method developed by Kohlberg is not appropriate for girls. The dilemmas, which are hypothetical and abstract, do not allow students to know the lives and personalities of the imaginary people, an essential element of female moral reasoning. Women, according to Gilligan, feel the need to know specific circumstances when making moral decisions. They are able to understand the causes and consequences that produce compassion and tolerance through context, two characteristics of the feminine sense of justice.

Subsequent study of girls' education has found that, in the fields of mathematics and sciences, girls seem to perform at a higher level in classrooms in which there are only girls, due to the different manner in which girls approach problems. This finding has been a boost to all-girls schools and has led some public schools to experiment with optional "girls only" sections of upper level math and science classes. (IDV, chapters 3, 4, 5)

In her book *Desarrollo moral y educación*, Maria Victoria Gordillo raises the question of whether or not girls need a different education than do boys. She suggests:

> What we expect of men and women as persons is the same: we expect them (both) to be just and at the same time to care for others; to be strong yet delicate; capable of dispassionate reasoning and affective intuition. However, we cannot overlook the obvious fact that boys and girls frequently have different orientations, and could be helped by different types of guidance.[12]

The question of what type of character education is most effective in modern America has not been resolved even now, at the beginning of the twenty-first century. The demands of the modern workplace and the failure of young people to meet them have provoked an on-going examination of the academic curriculum, but character education has not been able to come to a satisfactory redefinition in response to the moral dilemmas that modernity has provoked. This is apparent not only from the number of widely divergent theories that have been espoused within the last 40 years, but also from the number of methodologies that have been implemented and then discarded. Theory after theory has been put into practice only to be replaced because none has been able to instill lasting positive social attitudes in students.

Character education is in crisis but it is one that can be quieted by examining it piece by piece, reviewing the basic tenets upon which teaching for good character has been built in the past, and looking for alternative options both in theory and in practice. Character education will once again become a vibrant part of American education when we discover another foundation, one that has not already been used and found inadequate. However, before turning to some possible solutions, it is important to study the originator of most contemporary thought regarding character education, John Dewey.

PART II
JOHN DEWEY

Dewey – the Man

The son of a Vermont farmer, John Dewey was born in Burlington, Vermont on October 20, 1859. In his book, *The Life and Mind of John Dewey,* George Dykhuizen says, "John Dewey ... is a homespun, almost regional character. To this day, on meeting him, one would imagine oneself talking with a Vermont countryman."[1] In 1875, sixteen year-old Dewey entered the University of Vermont in Burlington; only Harvard, Yale, Brown, and Dartmouth predate it. Pursuing the classical liberal arts curriculum of his time, Dewey was one of ninety-four students taught by a faculty of eight professors. The University of Vermont faculty's confidence in the human mind and its right to think freely and independently earned the University the fame of being the most advanced in its thinking among New England universities. (LM, 10-11)

Although considered progressive among the then-existing universities, The University of Vermont of Dewey's time still reflected the "old American" Protestant attitudes of the New England region. Students were required to attend weekday morning services and, in addition to attending the church of their choice on Sundays, they were to keep a low profile socially so as not to violate the Sabbath. No alcohol was allowed on campus and students could smoke only in their rooms; smoking was forbidden in public areas. The University of Vermont also advised students not to frequent billiard saloons - the punishment was automatic expulsion. As the student handbook specified, "The conduct of the students toward all men is to be regulated by those plain rules of politeness, honor, and religion that are binding on every free and virtuous community."(LM, 9)

During his college years Dewey continued the religious practice that he had begun as a young boy under his mother's guidance. By the time he was old enough to enter college, however, he was practicing a type of liberal evangelism rather than the pietistic religion he had learned from his mother. Liberal evangelism encouraged its faithful to read and interpret the Bible intellectually, in light of their personal experience. Dewey's rational approach to religion continued for many years beyond his university experience. According to Dykhuizen, Dewey even speaks of a "mystical" experience while teaching in Oil City, Pennsylvania. This experience removed his recurring doubt about his sincerity while praying. A friend of Dewey's quotes him as saying, "I've never had any doubts since then, nor any beliefs. To me faith means not worrying ... I claim I've got religion and that I got it that night in Oil City."(LM, 22) In any case, Dewey continued to maintain his church membership for twelve more years.

Later, during graduate studies at Johns Hopkins (1882-1884), Dewey discovered Hegelianism, which tempered the Christian dualism he found disturbing even in liberal evangelism. This dualism included the opposition of the lower life of the flesh to the higher life of the spirit and the contrast between the person one is now and the perfection one ought to achieve in Christ. Although Dewey ultimately breaks with religion, many scholars attribute it to earlier experiences under his mother's tutelage rather than to his uneasiness with dualism. Dewey's "The Place of Religious Emotion" says, "Religious feeling is unhealthy when it is watched and analyzed to see if it exists, if it is right, if it is growing..."[2] Dewey's final break with religion, however, was intellectual and philosophical rather than emotional or a result of mystical considerations. After leaving religion behind, Dewey first embraced absolute idealism and its emphasis on the continuity of existence. Later he was to embrace humanistic naturalism, which stresses the continuity between man and nature.

Dewey's first job was a teaching position, typical of college graduates of his times. He did not stay in Burlington, however. Instead, he took a position in a school run by an aunt of his in Oil City, Pennsylvania. He stayed there from 1879-1882.

In 1881, toward the end of his stay in Oil City, Dewey sent two articles to the *Journal of Speculative Philosophy*, asking the editor, W. T. Harris, to review them. At the same time he asked Harris for advice concerning further studies in philosophy, which he had begun studying during his senior year of college. As a result of the encouragement he received from Harris, Dewey entered the newly founded Johns Hopkins University in 1882. Two years later, in 1884, he defended his doctoral dissertation, "The Psychology of Kant."(LM, 53)

In 1884, Dewey also accepted a position at the University of Michigan, where he met Harriet Alice Chipman, who was later to become his wife. Alice's grandparents had taken her into their home after the early death of her parents. Her personality reflected the influence her grandfather, an independent thinker who encouraged his granddaughter to be independent and self-reliant. Before attending the University of Michigan, Alice had studied at the Baptist Seminary in her hometown of Fenton, about forty miles from Ann Arbor. Alice was a junior when Dewey arrived at the University of Michigan. After a short wait for financial reasons, they were married in 1886 and eventually had five children. Dewey taught philosophy at the University of Michigan from 1892-1904, which included a year's stay at the University of Minnesota.

In 1905, on the go once more, Dewey moved his young family to the newly created University of Chicago. He had been appointed Head of the Philosophy

Department, which initially combined Psychology and Education. Under his leadership, however, the University created a separate department for education, and Dewey was appointed its head as well.

It was during this period that Dewey and his wife founded the Elementary School. The school later became known as The Chicago Laboratory School. The Laboratory School was "intended to test not only his pedagogical theories but his philosophical and psychology theories, the assumption being that the consequences of an actively oriented, empirically based, socially concerned philosophy would reveal themselves most directly in education."[3] After disputes with the President of the University of Chicago over management of the Laboratory School, Dewey left Chicago for New York City and Columbia University. There he taught philosophy and education. He remained at Columbia University until his retirement in 1930.

Although influenced by the writings of Hegel during his university career, Dewey's association with the founders of Pragmatism, J. Sanders Peirce and William James, was a much greater influence in his philosophical development. Referring to James, Dewey wrote that he was the "one specific philosophic factor that entered into my thinking so as to give it a new direction and quality."[2] Dewey developed his own version of Pragmatism, which he dubbed *Instrumentalism*. Instrumentalism viewed human values and ideals in terms of the biological and cultural environments in which individuals live. Instrumentalism focused mainly on the biological subject and the cultural environment.

Dewey's philosophy eliminated the supernatural and thus a metaphysical explanation of life; the development of Instrumentalism signaled his definitive break with religion. He also based his theories of social reconstruction and education on Instrumentalism. Dewey was to rework and rethink his philosophical premises continually throughout his life to the point that in 1939 he was able to write that "he might appear to be unstable, chameleon-like, yielding one after another to many diverse and even incompatible influences."[3] Dewey felt, however, that the discontinuity evident in his thought was a natural part of his own personal growth.

His stay at Columbia included a 5-month trip to Japan during a sabbatical leave from 1919 — 1921. There he gave a series of lectures entitled "The Position of Philosophy at the Present: Problems of Philosophic Reconstruction." Afterwards, the Deweys traveled to Mainland China, where he taught at the National University of Peking for two more years.(LM, Ch. 10)

Dewey wrote most of his works on education while at the University of Chicago, but by the end of his academic career he had published forty books and over seven hundred articles. The best known are "My Pedagogic Creed" (1897), *The School and Society* (1899), and "Democracy in Education" (1903). His works published during his Columbia years include *Ethics*, with James Tufts in 1908, *Human Nature and Conduct* in 1925, and *A Quest for Certainty* in 1929. In 1916 Dewey wrote *Democracy and Education*, in which we can find the clearest exposition of his educational philosophy. It contains Dewey's conception of democracy not only as a political system, but also as a "form of social life, and education as a social process nurturing the continual social, intellectual, and aesthetic growth of individuals, the continuing renewal and regeneration of society."(ME, 171) Dewey continued to write about these ideas until his death, using them extensively in formulating educational reforms.

In keeping with his concern for social reform, Dewey participated in many civic organizations, such as the American Federation of Teachers, the American Association of University Professors, and the Progressive Education Association. He was named Honorary President of the National Education Association in 1932. The University of Paris awarded Dewey a *honoris causa* degree in 1930, as did Harvard in 1932.(173)

From 1930 to 1939, Dewey retained the position of Professor Emeritus of Philosophy in Residence at Columbia. In 1939 he asked to have his position changed to simply Professor Emeritus of Philosophy, thus remaining in the university environment until he was seventy-eight years old. He continued to write until his death on June 1, 1952, at the age of ninety-two. (LM, 14, 15)

Chapter 1

Human Nature

To best understand John Dewey's philosophy of education, we need to study it from within his own philosophical framework. To do this, we will study two concepts that are basic to his theory — the social nature of human beings and his theory of inquiry. Afterwards, we will turn to Dewey's plan for American education.

The Social Essence of Human Nature

For Dewey, human nature is fundamentally social in origin. He maintained, "Association in the sense of connection and combination is a 'law' of everything known to exist."[1] Human association was so essential for Dewey that he did not consider the question of how association comes about an intelligent one. If human beings are "not bound together in associations, whether domestic, economic, religious, political, artistic or educational," he said, "[they] are monstrosities.[2]

In Dewey's philosophy, self-reflection does not play as important a role as self-understanding or self-awareness. The individual discovers a progressively greater self-awareness only through social living and interacting with others. Dewey writes in *Ethics* (1908) that "apart from the social medium, the individual would never 'know himself'; he would never become acquainted with his own needs and capacities.[3] On Dewey's view, individuals become familiar with their developing selves only indirectly. As he wrote, individuals are "incomplete without a social component, and [they] develop into what they are — individual members of groups as socially-grounded selves — in the ongoing process of living in a social environment."[4]

Dewey's understanding of self-awareness is central to his notion of social reform and the role that education plays within it - all individuals have a fundamental debt to the society in which they live, and they must repay it by advancing the common good.[5] Dewey argues that individual members of society must recognize their dependency on the social inheritance that they share. Since the influences of the social environment produce the "self," he concludes that if a person were born and raised in a different time and place, that individual would be essentially different. Even though genetically the same, the social influences would be distinct, thus making him a different individual.[5]

Dewey claims that knowledge of what is good in a given society is determined by what is familiar. In *Democracy and Society* he says, "What is strange or foreign ... tends to be morally forbidden and intellectually suspect."[6] The barrier thus raised between the individual and what is perceived as foreign encourages individual passivity and makes social reform difficult. He wrote in *Nature and Conduct,* "Ways of belief, of expectation, of judgment and attendant emotional dispositions of like and dislike are not easily modified after they have taken shape."[7] Therefore, anyone challenging what is familiar will necessarily encounter resistance, something any social reformer must keep in mind when trying to put needed social reform into practice.

Dewey's conviction that human nature has its origin in social interaction leads to his rejection of the idea that human nature can be understood in and of itself. He says that human nature can develop only within a social context. In 1939 Dewey wrote in *Freedom and Culture,* "The idea that human nature is inherently and exclusively individual is itself the product of a cultural individualistic movement."[8] Our sociability, says Dewey, is an essential part of us. Not only is it essential, sociability also defines individual personhood. Individuals cannot be correctly understood in isolation either by themselves or by others, for individuals develop a sense of self only through society and social interaction. "Our sense of our own personality is largely a looking-glass phenomenon," he says. "We form ideas, our estimate of ourselves and self-respect in terms of what others think of us, in terms of the way in which they treat us."[9] Dewey does admit that everyone wants to act independently at times, but he writes in *Democracy and Education* that individuals are mainly interested in "entering into the activities of others and taking part in conjoint and cooperative doings." (DE, 28) Individuals want to participate in society, he asserts, because they can come to know and understand themselves only in this way.

Put in educational terms, society is *the* character trainer for Dewey. Society molds individual members by encouraging some behaviors and discouraging others. Social environments lead "developing selves" to identification with the values and goals considered important by that society. These ideas define the purpose of education and its importance in Dewey's theory of social reform.

Another important mark of the social nature of human beings, scientific inquiry, plays a critical role in Dewey's educational philosophy. The principle of scientific inquiry, or the pattern of inquiry, says Dewey, is the basis of all human action. He holds that the interplay of man's social nature and the pattern of inquiry constitute the whole of the human being.[10]

The Pattern of Inquiry

Dewey's theory of the pattern of inquiry finds its origin in his definition of human nature. At the same time that individuals develop within a social environment and gradually acquire self-knowledge, Dewey maintains that each individual becomes aware of the fact that human actions, too, always take place within social contexts. Life itself acquires meaning only when viewed as a social reality. Actions, says Dewey, cannot be correctly understood in isolation, or when viewed as individual acts performed by individual persons. In 1922, after returning from China, Dewey wrote that "...conduct is always shared ... it *is* social, whether good or bad."[11]

For Dewey, life is a series of disequilibria and rediscoveries. Because of our potential for learning, these experiences can also be a process of growth - of uncovering connections and relationships and of finding more meaning in life.[12] Dewey was also convinced that the correct use of scientific inquiry, problem solving, was essential for personal fulfillment and for the advancement of society. Problem solving promotes individual and social growth, needed to overcome outdated modes of behavior and to change anachronistic social structures. In social terms, an attitude of problem solving allows humans to use inquiry in order to address shared problems.[13]

The process of problem solving applied to social issues involves five stages. During the first stage of inquiry society is functioning well and individuals have no difficulties to overcome. Dewey affirms that there is "no problem or difficulty in the quality of the experience that presents itself to provoke reflection."[14]

Problems begin to appear in the second stage of inquiry. Dewey says that activity should stop at this point because individuals begin to experience confusion or ambiguity. He describes a typical stage two situation in this way: "perplexity, confusion, doubt, due to the fact that one is implicated in an incomplete situation whose full character is not yet determined."(DE, 157)

During this stage of inquiry the individual either does not understand the meaning of the situation, or he does not know what to do. Now the individual's feelings of insecurity develop into thought, and he can formulate a hypothesis of the nature of the problem. This step is crucial because when the individual defines a difficulty that he feels, he now has a problem that he can solve. Insecurities can be resolved when difficulties are understood as problems. The goal of stage two, however, is not the resolution of the problem, but rather "an intellectualization of the difficulty or perplexity that has been felt into a problem to be solved."[15] During this stage Dewey cautions against the natural tendency to attempt to solve the problem before having defined it. He says that action should be suspended until the fifth stage, when the action taken is the fruit of careful previous analysis.

Stage three in Dewey's pattern of inquiry is a time of observation and investigation. Thought during this stage uses the definition of the problem formulated in stage two as the basis for its work. This is a speculative stage, where the individual formulates one or more solutions to the problem, taking into account what is stable and unchangeable as well as elements that can be modified or replaced.

After having formulated several possible solutions to the problem in stage three, the individual tests each idea mentally to foresee the consequences of each solution in stage four. After evaluating all of the solutions, the most adequate ones are moved into the fifth stage for further consideration as hypothetical solutions.

It is only during the fifth and final stage of the problem solving process that the individual is able to act. Until now the reasonable alternatives were considered only mentally. Stage five is the time to complete the process of analysis. Armed with the solution or solutions considered adequate to solve the problem, the individual now tests them by putting them into action. If the selected solution works, that is, if it solves the problem and brings society and the individual back to a state in which society is functioning well and individuals have no difficulties to overcome, the individual reverts to stage one, ready to take up the problem solving process again as soon as ambiguity or confusion is experienced.

As Dewey's pattern of inquiry suggests, individual human fulfillment is the fruit of active participation in reconstructive attempts at overcoming problems. Dewey does not limit his use of the pattern of inquiry to solving an individual's problems, however. He also applies it to larger, more global social problems, confident that the pattern of inquiry is the best tool to reconstruct our social praxis.

In brief, for Dewey, human nature is defined by and developed within society and under its tutelage. Individuals discover their personal identity and meaning in life through the demands of society and the adjustments that it requires of them, facing and solving the problems that social life presents. These problems can be as limited as an individual's personal states of insecurity, or as broad as social insecurity in global situations. In order to solve problems in either of these arenas, individuals must choose the best solution. The pattern of inquiry provides part of the answer to the question of which action is the best solution, but it does not answer the entire question.

One important issue remained, however, that Dewey could not resolve by means of the pattern of inquiry. This was the important problem of determining the nature of the good. Dewey sensed that this would have profound consequences in sorting out the best solutions to problems that he formulated through the pattern of inquiry and so he turned his attention to developing a theory of morality.

Chapter 2

Morality & Growth

Morality

Dewey's theory of morality is naturalistic — by the time he turns his attention to this issue, he has discarded any kind of religious guide in this area. His theory of morality rests upon his understanding of the social nature of the human being and the application of scientific inquiry to the pursuit of good conduct. "Ethics is the science that deals with conduct, in so far as this is considered as right or wrong, good or bad."[1] He felt that the scientific method of inquiry should be applied to ethics as well as individual or social problems. Throughout history, he asserts, there has always been a close relationship between ethical behavior and science — in their effort to solve the problem of obtaining enough food to feed a community, for example, people have caused scientific problems while trying to live moral lives. For its part, science has led to ethical problems, such as the problem of preserving the ecological environment.[2]

The Social Aspect of Morality

Since human conduct is essentially social, morality has a fundamentally social nature. In *Human Nature and Conduct* he claims that this is true "not because we ought to take into account the effects of our acts upon the welfare of others, but because of facts. Others do take into account what we do, and they respond accordingly."[3] Our actions interface with the actions of others and, as a result, we can do harm or fail to do good.

This thesis is the foundation of Dewey's ethics of service. In 1897 he wrote in "My Pedagogic Creed" that "the child is born with a natural desire to give out, to do, and that means to serve."[4] However, unless encouraged by the social environment, this innate spirit of service will not flourish. Dewey felt that the society of his time did little to foster this natural desire to serve. For Dewey there was only one response to the situation and for him, the response was obvious: inherited morality must change. In 1932 he wrote in *Ethics* that society needs a "working theory of morals" to provide the tools for reforming inherited moral theories that advance predetermined rights and wrongs.[5] Dewey argued that the moral system of his time was based on personal feelings, and therefore it could never foster an ethic of service. Service, he claimed, is not focused inwardly, on the individual person, but rather it looks beyond the individual to what can be done for others. He says as much in *The Moral Principles of Education* when he affirms that morality needs to "shift the center of ethical gravity from absorption which is selfish to service which is social."[6]

Dewey accused personal morality as he understood it of being isolationist and concerned strictly with one's own development. It was a barrier, he said, to developing a socially moral self, and was no longer sufficient in the modern world, which is essentially interpersonal. He wrote in *Ethics* (1932) "to attain personal morality in an age demanding social morality, to pride one's self upon results of personal effort when the time demands social adjustment is utterly to fail to apprehend the situation."[7] Dewey was convinced that each person's moral duty was to make the world better by contributing to the common good, and he was equally convinced that a morality based on personal development would lead to social indifference. An ethics of service would naturally lead members of society to a new involvement in social affairs and a greater commitment to the common welfare. When freed from personal morality, he declared, individuals could concentrate on social problems and dedicate themselves to bettering society for the benefit of all. "I doubt," he wrote in *Moral Principles in Education*, "whether a more momentous moral fact can be found in all human history than just this separation of the moral from other human interests and attitudes, especially from the economic."[8]

To reach a higher level of morality through an ethics of service, society must create a social environment that will support a higher level of morality. In his 1947 article "Liberating the Social Scientist", Dewey wrote, "Just as physical life cannot exist without the support of a physical environment, so moral life cannot go on without the support of a moral environment."[9] The members of society who are moral reformers will bring about this new moral environment able to foster and support an ethics of service. It is the duty of moral reformers to do this. Their contribution to the common good is to call the attention of others to the need of an ethics of service.[10]

Moral Inquiry

Human beings find meaning in their lives by resolving the problems they face. For Dewey, determining what is morally good is much like the process of acquiring self-knowledge through social interaction. Just as solving the problems of life gives life itself meaning, applying the pattern of inquiry to situations that demand a moral response will yield what is good in morally confusing situations. As a result, Dewey's moral theory has several distinctive characteristics.

Moral Laws

The first is that all moral laws are hypotheses to be tested, in the same way that solutions to problems are initially hypotheses to be tested. As in problem solving where one does not first decide upon a solution and then seek the means to justify it, in moral inquiry one does not first set a moral end and then search for the means to reach it. In *The Quest for Certainty: a Study of the Relation of Knowledge and Action*, Dewey wrote that a moral law is "a formula of the way to respond when specified conditions present themselves. Its soundness and pertinence are tested by what happens when it is acted upon."[11]

Dewey's main objection to the inherited morality found in American society was that it seemed to have predetermined goals. It focused too much on the individual person and gave very little importance to the individual's social responsibilities. This attitude created a barrier that kept individuals from creating the personal habits and social institutions essential for transforming society. Social transformation was, for Dewey, a primary goal of social life. In *The Quest for Certainty: A Study of the Relation of Knowledge and Action* he continues, "past experiences are significant in giving us intellectual instrumentalities ... They are tools, not finalities."[12]

Inherited Morality

Another important feature of Dewey's theory of moral inquiry is the attention it pays to the relationship between the means used to attain good moral behavior and the end of moral inquiry, good moral behavior. Within moral inquiry the role played by accepted morality is analogous to the role played by previous solutions in the process of problem solving. Just as current social situations can be used as the occasion for social reform, so past morality has value when viewed as a springboard to future moral hypotheses. When morality becomes outmoded, individuals should use it to discover a new morality, a new moral solution. Dewey explains the process in "Theory of Valuation" like this, "Every condition that has to be brought into existence in order to serve as a means is, in that connection, an object of desire and an end-in-view, while the end actually reached is a means to future ends as well as a test of valuations previously made."[13] The means and the end are the same thing, simply functioning in different manners. "Means and ends are two names for the same reality," he wrote in *Human Nature and Conduct*, "the terms denote not a division in reality but a distinction in judgment."[14]

Open-mindedness and Tolerance

Another distinctive element of moral inquiry is that differences of opinion in moral matters should not only be anticipated, but should also be accepted. Moral solutions are not predetermined, since the hypotheses forwarded to solve moral problems can be as varied as the individuals who postulate them. Consequently, open-mindedness and tolerance are essential to moral inquiry, because they encourage accepting differing moral views of the same situation as equally valid. Thus, Dewey says, experimentation, pluralism, and tolerance go hand-in-hand. These tools permit individuals in a democracy to appreciate the intelligence and personality of others, even if they hold opposing views. (ELW, 329)

Furthermore, Dewey considered all actions moral. "Morals is not a theme by itself," he wrote in "What I Believe" (1930), "because it is not an episode nor department by itself. It marks the issue of all converging forces of life."[15] As is true of life itself seen from Dewey's point of view, his moral scheme is a continuing process. Therefore, individuals must continually renew their moral goodness. In *Reconstruction of Philosophy* Dewey explains the fluidity of moral goodness by saying, "the bad man is the one who no matter how good he has been, is beginning to deteriorate, to grow less good. The good man is the man who no matter how morally unworthy he has been is moving to become better."[16]

Dewey determines morality by using the same paradigm that he uses when determining what human nature is - moral problems are resolved by analyzing them in a way that benefits other members of society. Dewey's theory of morals is an essentially fluid one. It is the same sense of movement that is also at the heart of Dewey's conception of society, the human person, and the purpose of life, which Dewey sums up in one word - growth.

Theory of Growth

The Deweyan concept of growth is important if we are to understand what he means by character training. Growth is a cornerstone in his educational philosophy, because Dewey claims that the entire purpose of education is growth. Finally, it is the last of the basic tools needed to understand Dewey's notion of how to educate, (based on human nature), what to teach as good, (based on his moral theory), and what character training is (based on his principle of growth).

Moral Growth

Because of Dewey's conception of human nature, human beings need a social environment in which the self can develop. In order to understand Dewey from within his own theoretical framework, we must understand what he means by the term development. The question of what life's goal is, for example, is a simple one for Dewey - growth. However, as in the areas of human nature and morality, in which he departed from "inherited morality and customs," his definition of growth also departs from what might commonly be assumed its definition.

Dewey holds that traditional society interprets growth as self-realization based upon a pre-established ideal found outside the self. Therefore, in 1923, Dewey could write in *Self-Realization as the Moral Ideal* that "within the framework of inherited modes of thinking, self-realization is directed by an effort to model the self upon characteristics which are predetermined and fixed."[17] This concept limits individual growth to the subjective assumption of objective qualities foreign to the individual, and makes the self similar to the ideal. Therefore, growth "within the inherited modes of thinking" means that all individuals acquire identical traits, causing a certain amount of homogeneity within society.

For Dewey, however, the purpose of life is the continuous reconstructive process of self-realization, which he contrasts with the identification of self with an extrinsic ideal. His idea begins by rejecting the inherited definition of growth, explicitly stating that the process of growth does not have a predetermined or fixed goal towards which it tends. Dewey believed that "growing, or the continuous reconstruction of experience is the only end."[18] In *Reconstruction of Philosophy* he provides yet another exposition of the meaning of growth: "the end is no longer a terminus or limit to be reached. It is the active process of transforming the existent situation, not perfection as a final goal. But the ever-enduring process of perfecting, maturing, refining is the aim of life."(181)

The Principles of Continuity of Experience and Interaction

Personal growth, he affirms, includes two factors. The first is the principle of continuity of experience. This principle states that present experience not only links experiences of the past to those of the future by means of the present, but it also implies that past experiences have the effect of modifying the character of possible future ones by contributing past influences. It is interesting to note the parallel roles of past experience in social transformation, past morality in the construction of new moral solutions, and past experience in the growth process.

The second principle involved in personal growth is the principle of interaction, which emphasizes the interplay that takes place between the objective or environmental conditions of experience and the individual or internal conditions of experience. Without the interplay between external and internal conditions of experience, which influence the individual's interpretation of the social milieu, personal growth cannot occur. This principle of interaction explains the gradual understanding of one's place in society and the gradual increase in one's ability to act within society and improve it.

There is one difficulty inherent in Dewey's concept of growth that must be acknowledged, however. Dewey himself addressed it in order to make his concept clearer: the possibility of growth that does not favor positive moral character or positive social participation. In 1920 Dewey had defined growth as "the active process of transforming the existent situation."(*Reconstruction and Philosophy*, 181) Given that definition, it would seem that the process of transformation could be directed either in a positive direction, thus increasing self-realization, or in a negative direction, resulting in a decline in selfhood. In response to these criticisms, Dewey argued in *Experience and Education* that only those experiences in which both the principle of continuity and the principle of interaction are present are growth experiences. He went on to explain that the presence of these two principles creates the possibility of future positive growth or self- realization. He was careful to clarify, however, in keeping with the indeterminacy of the growth process, that the growth he had in mind is not controlled by previous determinations. Growth caused by the principles of continuity of experience and interaction could either continue along the same lines or could take a turn along different lines.[19]

Accordingly, Dewey's scheme does not include negative growth. In *Experience and Education*, Dewey uses the example of an accomplished pickpocket to make his notions clear. An accomplished pickpocket does not grow through the experience of pick pocketing, even though he may have a high level of pick pocketing expertise. One of the essential ingredients of growth experiences, the principle of interaction, is absent in the pickpocket's trade. Dewey holds that any activity not contributing to the improvement of society does not possess the principle of interaction, and thus cannot be a growth experience. Acts such as pick pocketing, which narrow or disintegrate the self, cannot be defined as growth experiences. (*EE*, 19-24)

How Growth Takes Place

Having clarified the nature of growth experiences, Dewey goes on to describe the two phases in which growth occurs. The differences between them are a faithful reflection of Dewey's theory of the individual's relation to society. The first growth phase is one of increased control of the situation in which the individual exists. A good example would be the experience of learning a skill, which would allow more control over work possibilities and more opportunities to contribute to the common good. Another example could be the improvement of health conditions that result in better sanitation, a good affecting all members of society.

The second phase in the growth process involves increased meaning. Individuals in contact with those who think differently than themselves find new meanings in life's circumstances and thus grow in this second phase. Dewey considered the discovery of divergent interpretations of the same social situation to be the "greatest of human goods."[20]

The purpose of life is individual social growth. Dewey always imagined individuals essentially as members of society, indebted to their social environment for the creation of their personal self. Therefore, he also placed individual social growth in relation to the subsequent growth of society as a whole, not merely of the individual. This stress on the social consequences of individual growth implies once again that individuals have a moral obligation to contribute to the common good, an obligation to act out the good they acquire through growth. If the betterment of society requires continual change or reconstruction, then, according to Dewey, continual moral betterment through growth is a fundamental requirement of those who make up society.

For Dewey, everyone is obliged to contribute to the common good because, although humankind changes with a changing world, there are some basic human needs that do not change. Dewey writes of a "basic identity of human nature" in *Human Nature and Conduct* [21], and *Does Human Nature Change?* Describing some basic human needs, he wrote "I would mention as examples the need for some kind of companionship; the need for exhibiting energy ... the need for both cooperation and emulation of one's fellows for mutual aid ... the need to lead and the need to follow, etc."[22]

The Old Habitual Self and the New and Moving Self

Moral growth aims at the reconstruction of what he terms the "habitual self." Dewey argues that everyone has the moral obligation to fulfill the needs of human nature in order to foster the purpose of human life, that is, growth. In *Reconstruction in Philosophy* Dewey wrote that "[g]rowth is the only moral end …the process of growth, of improvement and progress … becomes the significant thing."[23] He explains that the habitual self is developed by forming habits as solutions to previous problems. These habits become outdated and in keeping with social reconstruction and personal growth, need to be replaced or reconstructed.

In *Ethics* (1932), Dewey describes the process of reconstructing habits and the two ways in which this relates to the self. First, reconstruction reveals the identity of the present self because it uses habits already acquired and used. Second, and simultaneously, reconstruction creates the future self by forming new habits to use in new situations. Dewey calls this new self the "new and moving self." Each time one act is chosen over another, the decision is not simply one of what to do, but is, in actuality, the determination of what type of person one wants to be and also the decision of the amount and direction of growth that will occur. For Dewey, the relationship of the "old habitual self" and the "new and moving self" is at the heart of moral development. The "old habitual self" is the basis for the moral inquiry that must take place to provide direction and quality for moral growth, aiming at the "new and moving self." Dewey's theory of moral growth contains no rules or absolutes. Ends are discovered within the process of moral reconstruction, just as they are discovered in the process of social reconstruction.

Moral Taste
    Dewey does admit, however, that growth needs direction, if not goals. Growth should be aimed at the betterment of the individual and of society. In order to discern which of all possible actions will produce positive growth, Dewey writes that individuals need to cultivate good moral judgment, which he calls "taste."

> One may say that the formation of taste is the chief matter wherever values enter in, whether intellectual, esthetic or moral... The formation of a cultivated and effectively operative good judgment or 'taste' is the supreme task set to human beings by the incidents of experience."[24]

For Dewey, the interaction between intelligence and experience provides all the guidance needed to develop taste; any criterion outside of experience is not valid or necessary in the development of taste. External criteria that is not the result of an individual's experience cannot be discovered through the growth process, and is consequently not an appropriate guide for growth. In spite of this insistence upon the sufficiency of personal experience in guiding growth, Dewey did, in fact, in his life and in his writings, consider certain social values such as democracy, equality, and freedom essential, even though they may exist outside the individual growth process.

Chapter 3

Growth & Education

Immaturity and Maturity

The primary condition for growth in children is immaturity, which Dewey defines as "the ability to develop."[1] He does not relate childhood immaturity to the maturity of an adult, as if immaturity were a passing stage, attaining meaning by its inevitable move towards adult maturity. He rejects this dependency. He also rejects the idea of reaching an objective "mature" state because he says that, having achieved adult maturity, growth could come to a stop because the goal of mature adulthood would have been achieved. (DE, 47)

From Dewey's point of view, childhood experiences have independent merit because all experiences have meaning in and of themselves. To acquire meaning the experiences of children need not be related to an externally imposed ideal such as adult maturity, just as adult experiences have meaning without reference to those of childhood. Dewey also argues that growth continues throughout one's entire life, and that the adult as well as the child continues to grow.

Dependency and Plasticity

Childhood immaturity is composed of two basic elements: dependency and plasticity. Dependency is at one and the same time the child's social power and a symptom of its social helplessness. Children, Dewey says, enter into social relationships precisely by means of their helplessness, which reflects their innate sociability. A good example of this is crying. By crying and attracting the attention of adults, children enter into social relationships with them. Crying also compensates for children's inability to cope with the physical environment, alerting adults to the fact that they must care for and nurture them. Crying thus becomes one means by which children increase control over their circumstances.

Crying also enables children to contribute to the strengthening of the social environment in which they live by deepening the interdependence of children and adults within society. (DE, 47-8)

Plasticity, immaturity's second component, complements the social power of dependency. Whereas dependency is the capacity for social growth, plasticity is growth itself; the ability to learn from experience, to "retain from one experience something which is of avail in coping with difficulties of a later situation."(DE, 49) Plasticity is the power children have to modify actions on the basis of past experiences and to develop new habits or dispositions. Thus plasticity is the childhood version of the principle of continuity of experience, which Dewey requires in all growth experiences.

Habit, Habituation and Education

Plasticity helps to form two types of habits or dispositions in children: active habits and habituation. Habituation is the relatively passive process of adjustment to the environment, but without any interest in changing it. Although habituation cannot play an active role in growth, the active virtues use its passive quality of adaptation as leverage in the growth process. Dewey defines active virtues as "a form of executive skill, skill in doing," which allows the child an "economical and effective control of the environment."(DE, 51)

Now Dewey unites education and growth. Education, he says, is essentially teaching adjustments that increase the child's ability to cause future changes in the environment. In this way education coincides with the first phase of growth, increased control. In *Democracy and Education* he writes, "Education is not infrequently defined as consisting in the acquisition of those habits that effect an adjustment of an individual and his environment. The definition expresses an essential phase of growth."(51)

Education and growth are one and the same thing. To grow, one must have learned active habits, and learning itself implies growth. Dewey's concept of education does not have a fixed end toward which it tends, in the same way that growth is not growth "into" a predetermined ideal. Education, Dewey asserts, is characterized by indeterminacy. In *Democracy and Education* Dewey writes, "translated into its educational equivalents, this means that *(i)* the educational process has no end beyond itself; it is its own end; and that *(ii)* the educational process is one of continual reorganizing, reconstructing, transforming."(57) Education as growth lasts a lifetime, because life itself is a process of continual reorganization, reconstruction and transformation. Education in school contributes to growth by "organizing the powers that ensure growth. The inclination to learn from life itself and to make the conditions of life such that all will learn in the process of living is the finest product of schooling."(56)

One can now anticipate some of Dewey's recommendations for school reform, geared toward ensuring that education actually fulfill the essential needs of the social human nature and contribute to social reconstruction. Dewey advocated the abandonment of fixed and predetermined educational goals formulated by adults and based on their perception of what is good for children to learn. In light of Dewey's insistence on the value and importance of childhood experience, any education directed towards goals set by adults would not satisfy his definition of true education. It would be an obstacle to the growth process rather than a help along the way.

In summary, Dewey's educational theory is predicated on the notion that growth is intimately associated with education, this being the process of organizing children's ability to grow. Education allows children to learn how to direct their growth toward the common good. In *Democracy and Education* Dewey writes, "Education means the enterprise of supplying the conditions which insure growth, or adequacy of life, irrespective of age... Life has its own intrinsic quality and ... the business of education is with that quality."(56)

Education and Democracy

Dewey's writings on education are linked to and dependent upon his political philosophy, which revolves around social reconstruction. Were it not for the critical role that education plays in maintaining and developing democracy, Dewey might not have addressed education at all.

Social Reconstruction

Dewey maintained that, to effectively respond to an ever-changing world, society continually needs reconstruction. As a method of change, social reconstruction uses inquiry and problem-solving. Essentially, social reconstruction is problem-solving applied to society, where it is no longer one individual solving personal problems, but rather individuals addressing and solving social issues together in their neighborhoods, cities or country.

However, to have citizens capable of social reconstruction, society must provide an education that will teach them the skills needed to put social reconstruction into practice. Consequently, education is at the core of Dewey's conception of social reconstruction, since it teaches members of society the skills that they will need to accomplish social reform. The education envisioned by Dewey needs to cultivate habits that all citizens require. In his article "Education and Social Direction" Dewey wrote, "The unsolved problem of democracy is the construction of an education which will develop that kind of individuality which is intelligently alive to the common life and sensitively loyal to its common maintenance."[2] He realized that this vision of education required a radical change in the existing educational system, and he was a harsh critic of what he termed the "traditional" education of his times. On Dewey's view education, using the school as its tool, had to fulfill two tasks vital to social living: problem-solving and cooperative living.

Schools and Social Reconstruction

Schools as an institution of society are important in forming the democratic identity. Their first job is helping students develop as problem-solvers, teaching them how to think rather than what to think. Dewey wrote in "Education and Politics" that the task of teachers is to foster a scientific attitude in their students by cultivating "the habit of suspended judgment, of skepticism, desire for evidence, appeal to observation rather than sentiment, discussion rather than bias, inquiry rather than conventional idealizations."[3] This attitude, critical, scientific, and essential to the growth and continuity of society, is the basis for Dewey's social reform. If members of society are not educated within this spirit, they simply become habituated to society's norms and lack the active virtues essential for growth. Because of this, Dewey wrote in *Ethics* that "the cause of democracy is bound up with development of the intellectual capacities of each member of society."[4]

One of the most important ideas that schools should teach as part of the process of problem solving is that customs inherited from former generations should be used as the basis for change. They should not be considered the *status quo*. Thus, it becomes "the job of a progressive society's educational system to prepare future adults to use customs without being overcome by them."[5] Within the society envisioned by Dewey, this understanding of *custom* is important. Rather than tradition, citizens promote betterment and social growth by using the critical capacity that was fostered in them at school. The ultimate goal of democratic education is to produce citizens with sound judgment who can judge discerningly when faced with the problems that social life brings with it.

Dewey realized that his theory of growth, so crucial to his political philosophy, could not take root within an educational system based on fixed goals, and which viewed childhood as a step on the way to adulthood. This is precisely what Dewey criticized in "traditional" education, which he claimed developed qualities designed to produce successful adults. By not giving enough importance to children's innate immaturity, Dewey thought that traditional education limited students' imagination by forcing it into predetermined channels. Education must be seen from a different point of view, said Dewey, if it were to develop students' capacity to solve problems and not predetermine growth by external motivation. Growth and education must find their ends within the child's immediate experience in order to be faithful to Dewey's ideas.

The School's Curriculum

The curriculum came under immediate attack. In *The School and Society*, Dewey wrote, "There is the standing danger that the material of formal instruction will be merely the subject matter of the schools, isolated from the subject matter of life experience."[6] School subjects, he asserted, bore no connection to children's experiences outside the classroom. He further argued that traditional education placed "the center of gravity outside the child ... anywhere and everywhere you please except in the immediate instincts and activities of the child himself." Dewey's educational theory, designed to foster inquiry, used the child's personal experience as the basis for teaching and learning. "[The] primary root of all educational activity is in the instinctive impulsive attitudes and activities of the child ... [They] are the foundation stones of all educational method."(23, 81)

School has meaning for students when the curriculum corresponds to what is naturally appealing to them and when it is based upon daily life and interests. Curricula thus conceived are not typical of traditional education, which is a stiff and lifeless series of facts to memorize and repeat, having meaning only in the artificial environment of the school itself. Dewey's school curriculum linked learning to life. It was the occasion for solving problems relevant to the child's social environment. Dewey's school curriculum also gave the value to childhood that he felt had been robbed from it by previous educational traditions. "In this school the life of the child becomes the all-controlling aim," says Dewey. Writing about his Laboratory School at the University of Chicago in *The School and Society* he says, "All the media necessary to further the growth of the child center there. Learning? - certainly, but living primarily, and learning through and in relation to this living."(24)

The second task of education, in Dewey's scheme, is teaching students to live cooperatively as members of a group, working as a social unit rather than individually to accomplish tasks. Education is democracy's most important tool in helping students "take their own active part in aggressive participation in bringing about a new social order."[7] Dewey frequently said that schools are "the most far-reaching and the most fundamental way of correcting social evils and meeting social issues."[8]

The Democratic Classroom

To correct social evils, however, not only must the curriculum reflect student interests, but the classroom environment must also be democratic and the school itself should be the place where children practice social living. In a report he helped prepare for the New York and the Seabury Investigation Dewey wrote,

> In the first place the school itself must be a community life in all which that implies ... In place of a school set apart from life as a place for learning lessons, we have a miniature social group in which study and growth are incidents of present shared experience ... the learning in school should be continuous with that out of school. There should be a free interplay between the two ... isolation renders school knowledge inapplicable to life and so infertile in character."[9]

Dewey felt that traditional classroom instruction typically encouraged passivity, and so he advocated reform of traditional teaching methods. He felt that even if not expressly designed to do so, traditional teaching methods cultivated habituation to the *status quo* by treating children en mass and expecting all of them to learn the same facts and information. In "Social Purposes of Education" he also spoke of a systemic avoidance of criticism among educators. To remedy this, Dewey advocated a greater political consciousness in schools, giving students not only the ability to adapt to change, but also the power to shape and direct it, thus helping them become familiar with the underlying problems they would encounter as adults in local, state, and national politics.[10]

School Organization

Because of the way that schools were organized, Dewey felt that, without reform, schools could not be the training ground for intelligent participation in a democratic society.[11] Thus, the third aspect of Dewey's school reform dealt with procedures and the organizational structures. The way a school is organized and carries out its activities, he contended, determines the climate in which students learn socialization, one of education's primary goals. He criticized school authorities for keeping decision-making in their own hands, not allowing students to make decisions of importance. Because school imposed rules upon students, rules appeared to be arbitrary, and there was no real link between behavioral expectations in school and the expectations of children outside of school. To teach children the importance of their identity as members of society was, Dewey argued that students should have the opportunity to live and to work in a social environment from early childhood. He was convinced that this was the only way to produce the aggressive, inquiring citizens needed to guide society.

He set about formulating proposals for the school climate and organization that conformed to his ideas regarding the essential purpose of education. Dewey's reorganization began by replacing what he saw as an individualistic goal of traditional American education with the social goal demanded by social reconstruction.[12] Schools needed to be structured and to be run democratically.

> [W]hether this educative process is carried on in a predominantly democratic or non-democratic way becomes therefore a question of transcendent importance not only for education itself but for its final effect upon all the interests and activities of a society that is committed to the democratic way of life."[13]

He asserted that school is primarily a social institution in which the student emerges "from his original narrowness of action and feeling to conceive of himself from the standpoint of the welfare of the group to which he belongs.[14] Schools, after all, must be tools for the advancement of a thriving democracy. Authoritarian rather than democratic styles of leadership would be unable to provide an education capable of producing democratically minded students. Schools organized as communities, however, in which school life fostered social responsibility, could easily encourage the attitudes of social responsibility and participation that Dewey envisioned for democratic citizens.

> The primary business of school is to train children in cooperative and mutually helpful living, to foster in them the consciousness of mutual interdependence, and to help them practically in making the adjustments that will carry this spirit over into deeds ... reproduc[ing] on the child's plane the typical doings and occupations of the larger maturer society into which he is finally to go forth."[15]

Dewey envisioned schools organized as democratic communities that could teach students to participate in and to evaluate decision-making. The democratic spirit that Dewey imagined permeating schools would also help students learn that it is the responsibility of each member of society to be critical and aggressive in bringing about a new social order. In *School and Society,* Dewey termed the school climate an "embryonic social life."(SS, 19) In *Democracy and Education* he explained further; "education is a projection in type of the society we should like to realize, and by forming minds in accord with it will gradually modify the larger and more recalcitrant features of adult society."(DE, 26)

Chapter 4

Character Training

Character Formation and Society

Dewey begins his discussion of character formation in schools by noting that character formation is an integral part of a democratic education. Interestingly, in his writings on character formation Dewey does not descend to the detailed suggestions that he offers when addressing the nature and importance of science, the arts, or geography.

His conception of character itself and how he thinks it ought to be educated explain his lack of detail in this regard. In "Character Training for Youth," Dewey argues that character is composed of "all the desires, purposes, and habits that influence conduct... The mind of an individual, his ideas and beliefs, are part of character."[1]

One of Dewey's basic tenets is that society forms a child's self, his character, and his conduct. Since personality is the result of social interaction, good character springs from social involvement and is the result of membership in a social group. Dewey writes just this in "Character Training for Youth" when he says that "every influence that modifies the disposition and habits, the desires and thoughts of a child is a part of the development of his character." (CT, 187)

Since society, which includes influences other than schooling, molds character, Dewey felt that character formation can and should be carried out independent of formal schooling. He writes that character "is such an inclusive thing, the influences that shape it are equally extensive...the moral education of our children is in fact going on all the time, every waking hour of the day and three hundred and sixty-five days a year... In short, formation of character is going on all the time; it cannot be confined to special occasions." (CT, 186-87)

Major Influences in Character Formation

Dewey's list of the major influences in character formation is very enlightening. Of the four most significant factors in character formation, Dewey places schools that the bottom of the list. He does not think that school is an inappropriate environment for character education — he is simply convinced that schools have the least impact on young people. Social relations, the natural tendency to engage in common activities, and the family rank as the top three influences on Dewey's list.

Dewey writes in "Character Training for Youth": "the concrete state of social relations and activities is the most powerful factor in shaping character... because children have an innate tendency toward activity and some kind of collective association."(190, 192) Since society guides youth in such natural and unobtrusive ways, Dewey argues that indirect character education is much more effective than formal or direct instruction.

Because they do not preach or arouse student resistance, indirect influences have a more lasting impact than do schools. Dewey feels that this resistance is inevitable in formal instruction. "The friends and associates of the growing boy and girl," Dewey says, "what goes on upon the playground ... the books they read, the parties they attend ... their effect is all the greater because they work unconsciously when the young are not thinking of morals at all."(187)

Dewey places the family's influence on children under society's and friends' influence, but he does give special importance to the relationship children have with their parents. He cites the then-new science of psychology and its studies "with respect to how relations between persons - between parents with respect to each other and with respect to their offspring - affect character."(191) The relatively low rank that Dewey gives the family reflects the normative power that he attributes to the sanctions of social groups and their influence in determining what is good in society. Social sanctions, which include parental guidance, constitute the primary influences in a child's character.

Because character education takes place in social environments and because character education is one of society's main tasks, Dewey places society at the head of the list. Dewey claims that schools will be effective in character education insofar as they work in conjunction with society. Explaining why he gives such little credit to schools he says, "If I put the school fourth and last it is not because I regard it as the least important of factors in moral training, but because its success is so much bound up with the operation of the three others." (192)

Dewey's proposals for social change to promote better character reflect his preference for indirect character education. He also advocates an economy based on cooperation rather than competition. He says, "It is difficult to produce a cooperative type of character in an economic system that lays chief stress upon competition, and wherein the most successful competitor is the one who is the most richly rewarded and who becomes almost the social hero and model."(191) Although he does not give his new economic system a name, Dewey advocates guaranteeing useful work for all citizens, security for old age, decent housing, and educational opportunity for all children based on means other than money. Thus, says Dewey, society will reduce competition and foster cooperation.

Dewey's second suggestion to improve the character of American youth is better parent education. Parents who are aware of the impact that their actions have on their children will make sure that it is character building, he says. When they receive a more democratic education, parents will realize that their attitudes and reactions toward their children have a vital impact on the self-image that the young acquire. "There are still multitudes of parents," he writes, "who ... are totally unaware of the influences that are the most powerfully affecting the moral fiber of their children."(CTY, 191) Finally, Dewey advocates a more comprehensive program of free time activities, both in rural areas and in cities, where youth do not have places to congregate, or things to do. Dewey's last suggestions for social reform center on schools.

Character Education in Schools

Although Dewey placed schools at the bottom of the list, he spared no effort in suggesting ways to improve the character education that they did offer, precisely so that schools can play a more effective role in society's task of character formation. We must understand Dewey's conception of character education in schools, however, within the context of his goal of education in a democracy. His concerns regarding character education and education in general, revolve specifically around furthering democratic society. Dewey feels that education is one of the main tools with which to secure democracy's continuity. "Democracy has to be born anew every generation, and education is its midwife," he wrote in *The Need of an Industrial Education in an Industrial Society*.[2] For Dewey, character education was education in social living, preparation for participation in democracy.

In *Democracy and Education* Dewey wrote, "The moral and social qualities of conduct are, in the last analysis, identical with each other. The measure of the worth of the administration, curriculum, and methods of instruction of the school is the extent to which they are animated by a social spirit ... a permeating social spirit ... [is] effective moral training."[3] Since Dewey held that both morality and character are social, good character means better conduct as democratic citizens. Schools, therefore, must think of character education in terms of educating for citizenship, helping students recognize social relationships, and preparing them for leadership in society. He states this conviction clearly in *Moral Principals in Education*: "The school is fundamentally an institution erected by society to do a certain work, - to exercise a certain specific function in maintaining the life and advancing the welfare of society."[4]

Dewey also held that all education is moral education. "All the aims and values which are desirable in education are themselves moral," he explains in *Democracy and Education*. (DE, 369) Dewey's criticism of traditional education stems in part from the fact that "we have associated the term ethical with certain special acts which are labeled virtues and are set off from the mass of other acts, and are still more divorced from the habitual images and motives of the children performing them ... The moral has been conceived in too goody-goody a way."(MP, 285)

School as Community

Dewey's first concern was the environment of the school as a whole. He was convinced that a school's climate was its most valuable tool in character education. In *Moral Principles in Education* he called the school climate the "larger field of indirect and vital moral education ... through all the agencies, instrumentalities and material of school life." (MP, 268) Dewey's disapproval of didactic moral education highlights his conviction that effective moral education is carried out through the environment fostered within a school. "Formal instruction," he says, "has no great force in comparison with the indirect effect of conditions that are operating all the time in school and out." (CTY, 189)

Dewey insisted that schools be structured and organized as a community because character education was a natural part of the school's environment and the community spirit was the foundation for the moral importance of the school. According to Dewey, the most fundamental and important lessons that schools teach are lessons in how to live within society, how to cooperate, and how to develop a sense of responsibility for society. He even wrote in *Moral Principles in Education* that "apart from participation in social life, the school has no moral end nor aim."(MP, 190)

Teaching and Character

In his discussion of character education, Dewey takes a new look at the art of teaching. This time he concentrates not on technique, but rather on the place of teaching within character education. He encourages teachers to demonstrate a spirit of service while teaching, rather than advocating specific teaching methods. Here Dewey again takes up the theme of indirect versus direct moral education, making the distinction between teaching and forming. "Character, in short, is something that is formed rather than something that can be taught as geography and arithmetic are taught." He feels that direct instruction provides "ideas about morality" but does not necessarily improve conduct, which is the goal of character formation. "[I]t may be laid down as fundamental," he writes, "that the influence of direct moral instruction, even at its very best, is comparatively small in amount and slight in influence, when the whole field of moral growth through education is taken into account."(MP 268, 275)

In Dewey's opinion, traditional teaching fostered self absorption, exclusiveness, and competition among students, all of which can suffocate the spirit of cooperation needed in a democracy. By requiring all students to perform the same tasks, there is no opportunity for division of labor, no chance to do creative activities. He insisted on restructuring the classroom to promote active student participation in learning and character education by social interaction within a democratic environment. Dewey advocates "the introduction of every method that appeals to the child's active powers, to his capacities in construction, production, and creation, mak[ing] an opportunity to shift the center of ethical gravity from an absorption which is selfish to a service which is social."(MP, 277)

Character and Curriculum

Dewey's ideas for school reform also necessitated a second look at the curriculum in order to be effective in bringing character education into every aspect of school. Dewey felt that "in many respects it is the subject-matter used in school life which ... decides the general atmosphere of the school." His overriding concern with the social and moral implications of education can perhaps be most clearly seen in his rationale for specific course content. He writes that "a study is to be considered as a means of bringing the child to realize the social sense of actions. Thus considered it gives criterion for selection of material."(MP 278) All subjects, he felt, need to be taught in relation to the purpose of human life. Students are bored and uninterested if not taught in this way.

> When a study is taught as a mode of understanding social life it has positive ethical import. What the normal child continually needs is not so much isolated moral lessons upon the importance of truthfulness and honesty, or the beneficent results that follow from a particular act of patriotism, as the formation of habits of social imagination and conception." (MP, 283)

Dewey's emphasis on the social significance of curriculum led him to encourage the study of art, geography, and history. When writing about geography, he claims that the ultimate meaning of geography is not physical, but rather social and ethical. "The ultimate significance of lake, river, mountain, and plain is not physical but social," he says. "It is the part which it plays in modifying and directing human relationships." (MP, 285)

Dewey thought of all education in terms of its moral or character formation. He advocated furthering the socialization of students by means of every aspect of the school. He advocated designing curriculum to reflect the social significance of each subject, teaching in a spirit of service and revising the school climate so that students participate in democratic communities from an early age. Thus, he assumed, students learn the social and moral inquiry essential to continual reconstruction of a vibrant democracy.

Conclusion

John Dewey is legendary in American education. He is a seminal figure in the history of modern educational thought. Because of the great impact that Dewey has had on public education in the United States, educators need to look deeply into the philosophical assumptions that underlie his educational theories. Some of his ideas have far-reaching consequences. His concept of growth, for example, seems to be at odds with the goal that he sets for education — formation of democratic citizens. One can also wonder if good citizens would be even better citizens if they were encouraged to value intellectual pursuits in addition to socialization.

His concept of growth also seems at odds with an innate tendency observed by all teachers — students want be able to follow the teacher's discussion as she moves towards the goal or purpose of the lesson. Students frequently complain that a class seems pointless when they do not see its purpose. Education perceived as an end in itself does not inspire anyone. Dewey does not seem to realize that not only does he have goals for education, producing good democratic citizens, but that he wants the students of the United States to grow in a specific way so that they can later take leadership roles in the United States' democratic society.

Dewey's practical approach to education caught on very quickly, as did his idea that morality must be able to change with the times. Given the contemporary crisis in education in this country however, practical solutions can resemble band-aids more than real solutions to serious educational issues. In addition, since Dewey's era, our society has discovered some values that have stood the test of time and that are not simply the jumping board to a new morality.

PART III
ALASDAIR MACINTYRE

MacIntyre - the Man

Alasdair MacIntyre's writings in moral philosophy and its implications for character education provide a perspective on character and its formation that differs dramatically from that of John Dewey, offering intriguing alternatives for educators interested in fostering good character.

John Dewey thought and wrote within the framework of American Pragmatism. He formulated his ideas on character and its training within that tradition. In his proposals for character education, Dewey's goal was to prepare students for a world their parents had not experienced. Theirs had been a stable and predictable world, while Dewey's America was in a state of rapid transition, contrasting sharply with the nurturing, quiet life characteristic of American culture earlier in the nineteenth century.

Dewey tried to formulate a moral and educational philosophy that would prepare students for success in the modern world that was emerging. In the process, he rejected the character education and moral philosophy typical of the tranquility of a small town. He considered his philosophy to be progressive and forward looking, designed for the new way of living out American democracy. Dewey's goal was to produce citizens with moral criteria who would be in tune with the one thing that was constant in modernity - change.

Alasdair MacIntyre approaches the relationship of modern society to moral philosophy from a distinct vantage point. Rather than seeing modern society as key to moral philosophy as Dewey did, MacIntyre regards modern industrial societies and the liberalism that they espouse as destructive of morality. On his view, modernism and liberalism are the main obstacles to establishing a unified sense of purpose - Dewey's philosophy focused on cultivating a capacity for adaptation in keeping with the evolution of democratic society. Thirty-five years later, MacIntyre stands within the same American democracy and finds little in its liberalism to direct to those who live within it.

Alasdair MacIntyre was born on January 12, 1929 in Glasgow, Scotland. He describes his childhood as being a mixture of his grandparents' Gaelic oral traditions and pressure to prepare himself for the modern world in which his Gaelic roots no longer had meaning. In a 1994 interview he described the Gaelic tradition as one of "farmers, fishermen, poets, and storytellers, and what mattered were particular loyalties and ties to kinship and land. To be just was to play one's assigned role in the life of one's local community, and each person's identity derived from their place in the community, its conflicts and its arguments. The modern world was one of theories rather than stories, and its claims were those of universal, rational humanity." [1]

MacIntyre was educated in England, receiving his Bachelor of Arts from Queen's College, University of London, in 1949. He then received a Masters of Arts from Manchester University in 1951, and another from Oxford in 1961. By the time he moved to the United States in 1969, he had been a research fellow in Nuffield College, Oxford University from 1961-1962, a senior fellow on the Council for the Humanities at Princeton from 1962-1963, a fellow at the University College, Oxford University 1963-1966, and a professor of sociology at the University of Essex from 1966-1969.

His penchant for mobility did not stop when he arrived at Brandeis University in 1969 to teach History of Ideas until 1972. After spending one year as the Dean of the College of Liberal Arts at Boston University (1972-1973) and subsequently teaching philosophy and political science there, he was appointed Henry Luce Professor from 1980-1982 at Wellesley College. In 1982 MacIntyre accepted the position of W. Alton Jones Professor at Vanderbilt University. He left Vanderbilt in 1988 for Notre Dame University, where from 1988-1993 he held the Mahone/Hank Chair of Philosophy. This appointment came at approximately at the same time as his conversion to Catholicism. He taught at Duke University, North Carolina from 1993 until his return to Notre Dame, where he currently resides.

If MacIntyre's personal life is one of constant movement, his intellectual life is no less so. He began his academic career as a Marxist. In his search for an alternative to the post-Enlightenment, he moved from Marxism in the 1950s to analytical philosophy in the 1960s to Aristotelian philosophy in the 1970s, to Thomism in the 1990s.

Since 1972, however, the year he began to write *After Virtue*, two features of his thought have remained constant: his radical criticism of modern liberalism and his conviction that moral, political, and metaphysical problems can only be adequately stated and resolved within an Aristotelian framework.[2] He rejects liberalism but makes it an essential feature of his writings from the time of *After Virtue*.

As early as 1953, when he published *Marxism: an Interpretation*, MacIntyre was already trying to find a moral philosophy that would give back to human life the unity that he thought modern liberalism had destroyed. His way of doing this was to study ethics as an independent area of inquiry. He argued that a variety of moral beliefs existed, each valid in itself, and so he examined history and anthropology to learn more about the numerous moral practices and beliefs that guided human behavior. In *A Short History of Ethics* (1966) he wrote that moral concepts are developed within social life and form a foundational part of it.[3] At the same time that he recorded and described different moral schemes, however, he unwittingly found himself evaluating them. Without realizing it, he was judging them from his own moral standpoint. He wrote,

> I seemed to be asserting that the nature of moral community and
> moral judgment in distinctively modern societies was such that it was
> no longer possible to appeal to moral criteria in a way that had been
> possible in other times and places - and that this was a moral calam-
> ity! But to what could I be appealing, if my own analysis was cor-
> rect? [4]

By the time he published *After Virtue*, MacIntyre had answered his question
and had found the source of unity for which he had been searching. His redis-
covery of classical practical philosophy was a turning point in his intellectual
journey. Since then he has advocated a renewal of Aristotelian moral philosophy
and the rejection of liberalism.

In *After Virtue* MacIntyre discusses the fact that the modern conception
of morality has been reduced to the expression of subjective preferences, and
that consequently, no objective criteria can be available for comparison among
them. To counter this situation, MacIntyre advocates the Aristotelian concepts of
community, virtue, narrative, and tradition, all of which maintain that the good
life is achieved through the traditions and the history of each society; however,
the *télos* or ultimate goal, which defines the good life, transcends any particular
social customs. [5]

In his two of his major works since then, *Whose Justice? Which Rationality?* (1988) and *Three Rival Versions of Moral Inquiry* (1990), MacIntyre
refines some of the conclusions that he made in *After Virtue*. He also addresses
the problem of how to rationally recommend one tradition of thought over another, and asserts that no rational inquiry can exist outside of the standpoint of
some particular tradition. He recommends Thomism; it can resolve problems
recognized by liberal and Nietzschean philosophies in a way that neither liberalism nor Nietzscheanism can answer adequately from within their own traditions. [6]

Chapter 1
MacIntyre's Intellectual Framework

MacIntyre's endorsement of the Aristotelian virtue ethic sets him apart from most American philosophers. To understand why he endorses the Aristotelian alternative to liberalism, we need to look at the history of the enlightenment project and the specific defects MacIntyre finds in liberal moral philosophy.

Modern liberalism has its roots in the enlightenment project of the nineteenth century. Nineteenth century philosophers tried to discover a universal rational moral principle that they could remove from its historical and social context and whose validity could be proved to anyone. Although most of the philosophers agreed that such a moral principle existed, after studying the issue individually they found that they could not agree on the supporting arguments or on the conclusions to be drawn from this universal rational moral principle. The result was a splintering of liberal thought that has had far reaching consequences. The multiplication of moral options that appeared during the enlightenment did not remain theoretical for long. It quickly descended to the concrete moral behavior of the man on the street. In the post-enlightenment period today, a plurality of moral theories has continued to flourish. Liberal societies are not grounded in any one specific moral philosophy and cannot offer their members a coherent moral code to use in evaluating their own or others' behavior.

For MacIntyre, the first major defect of liberal moral philosophy is the lack of moral guidance found in liberal societies along with the multiplicity of moral options that seem to be acceptable. The American public expects its political figures to behave honestly in the public forum at the same time that they seem to accept as normal the possibility of less than honest behavior in the private lives of the same politicians.

This moral fragmentation is also an accepted part of life for many private citizens; people often experience contradictory moral expectations. A father who works for a large firm may find himself being dishonest in order to keep his job. If he discovers that his son has lied, however, he would probably try to explain to the child how important honesty is in life. In a liberal society each role that people play in life can have its own moral requirements that are not infrequently contradictory.

A second major problem that MacIntyre sees in liberal moral philosophy is the affirmation of justice as the highest moral virtue. Justice is the foundation of liberal societies, taking precedence over the understanding of what is good. For a liberal society to function well there is no need for a common understanding of the good. Furthermore, a liberal society requires its institutions to take a neutral stand in the interpretation of what is good, leaving the individual free to seek out and define the good as each one chooses. The American ideal of the "rugged individual" working out a place in the world independently of others fits into this liberal ideal perfectly. The fabric of our moral heritage has been woven by the belief that each person has a right to think and to act as he pleases; any infringement on this right to personal freedom is a major lack of justice. Americans often think of themselves as a nation of individuals standing side by side with breathing space in between them.

MacIntyre replies that, on the practical level, liberal societies deny their members the possibility of seeking the good at all. He maintains that if liberal thought had been successful, one would see a flourishing of individual projects in societies, each in search of the good. The fact is, he says, that there is no evidence of this in modern liberal societies. Members of liberal societies seem to be content with their role as consumers rather than innovators, proving that liberalism in fact denies the possibility of searching for the good.

> Liberalism, while imposing through state regimes that declare every-
> one free to pursue whatever they take to be their own good, deprives
> most people of the possibility of understanding their lives as a quest
> for the discovery and achievement of the good, especially by the way
> in which it attempts to discredit those traditional forms of human
> community within which this project has to be embodied."[2]

It seems that MacIntyre's evaluation of liberalism is validated by the daily reality of contemporary American life. In fact, one of the most urgent concerns of education and American society today is that young people have not been successful in determining what is good for them. The declining moral behavior of youth, the escalation of violence, adolescent pregnancy, a lack of regard for authority, and a general weakening of academic performance have all been attributed to the inability of young people to distinguish right from wrong.[3]

The Rediscovery of Virtue

MacIntyre stands among the few prominent American philosophers in his advocacy of the Aristotelian concept of the moral life as a viable solution to the moral dilemmas characteristic of our modern liberal society. We will now examine the Aristotelian concept of virtue and the good life that will serve us as the basis for a discussion of MacIntyre's contribution to contemporary moral philosophy.

Aristotle's Moral Scheme

In order to understand Aristotle's moral philosophy, we must first understand his concept of *teleology*. Aristotle believed that human beings have a distinctive end or *télos* to achieve. Stated in another way, each human being has a distinctive function to fulfill. Aristotle begins the *Nicomachean Ethics* by saying, "Every art and every inquiry, and similarly every action and pursuit is thought to aim at some good ... and for this reason the good has rightly been declared to be that at which all things aim."[4] Therefore, the most important questions anyone can ask are "What is the human good?" and "How can I attain that good?" Aristotle argued that the goodness specific to human beings is found within human nature and is embedded within each person. He argues in addition that we can attain the good by means of daily living. His ethics is one of discovering the basis of morality in the structure of human nature and within human activity.

Discovering the goal, end, or purpose of human life begins by making the distinction between *instrumental ends* used as means to achieve other ends, and *intrinsic ends*, which are sought for their own sake. The example of a doctor illustrates this distinction well. A doctor works to maintain and recover good health. A doctor wants to restore his patient's health, but for what purpose? Is health a good that we seek for its own sake - health for the sake of health - or do we seek health because by using it we can attain a higher sort of good, one that needs health as a means to attain it? Doctors (and patients) know very well that the good that we call health is one of the means we need to obtain other higher goods. Aristotle says that the same can be said of any other profession. He considered the goods for which we work professionally to be instrumental ends because we use them as the means to attain another end. Since we use the money we earn to buy food, and we eat the food we buy to stay healthy, and we use our health to go skiing, none of these can be the good that humans seek for its own sake. Aristotle says that there is one good that we do seek for its own sake - he calls it the *good of man*.[5]

To define *good* and to define the *good of man*, Aristotle looks at the role that function plays in determining goodness. He uses a hammer and a carpenter to prove his point. A hammer is good if it does what hammers are supposed to do. In the same way, a carpenter is good when he can fulfill the function of a carpenter. Aristotle says that there is a difference, however, between professional activity and activity as a human being. One can be a good carpenter and not be a good person, and one can be a good person and not be a good carpenter. Therefore, humans perform two types of functioning. One is a professional function, for example, the function of a carpenter. The other type of functioning is a purely human functioning. Aristotle initially concludes that living is the purely human functioning. He immediately notes, however, that simply living is not an activity unique to human beings. Plants and animals are also alive. Therefore, there must a type of life or way of being alive that is unique to human beings, and that type of life Aristotle says, is the rational life, lived in accordance with virtue.[6]

Having come to that conclusion, Aristotle next analyzes the human soul, since the soul is the source of rational life. The first thing to note is that the soul has two parts: the rational and the irrational. What kinds of activity does each part of the soul perform? Aristotle looks at human activity and notices that humans eat, sleep, reproduce, and grow. He correctly concludes that these functions are not unique to the human being, since both plants and animals do these things. Aristotle turns to the senses — we can see, hear, taste, and feel objects. Animals can also use their senses. We also have emotional responses that are reflected in the animal world. Aristotle is forced to admit that these types of activity are not uniquely human. Since the activities of the rational part of the soul (abstract thinking and the ability to make free choices) are the only activities that humans do not have in common with either plants or animals, Aristotle concludes that in order to lead a truly human life the rational part of the soul should govern the non-rational activity of the soul.

Nancy Sherman writes in *The Fabric of Character* "to act rightly is to act rightly in affect and conduct. It is to be emotionally engaged ... It is to reason and see in a way that brings to bear the lessons of the heart as much as the lessons of a calmer intellect."[7]

As mentioned above, a thing is said to be good in relation to how well it fulfills its function. Acts that are unique to humans are those that are rationally controlled. Therefore, humanly good actions are actions that are guided and controlled by reason. However, the irrational part of the soul, made of our desires and our appetites, is not governed inherently by any rational principle. It operates on the basis of attraction and repulsion. In fact, conflicts between the rational and irrational aspects of the soul give rise to moral questions and provide part of the subject matter of morality. Therefore desire and the appetites need the guidance of reason to assure their cooperation in morally good acts.[8]

Habit plays an important role in the process of guiding the appetites, the will and the intellect. Habits are those acts that, because of their repeated occurrence, have become stable dispositions of the soul that facilitate that action. Good habits are termed virtues because they facilitate good actions. There are two types of virtue: intellectual, which direct the intellect, and virtues of character (moral virtues), which perfect the will and the appetites. Virtue guides all of the faculties of the soul so that they function properly and so that they are directed toward the *telos*.[9] Morality consists of developing and exercising moral virtue, the result of which will be right thinking, right choices and right conduct.

Virtue, then, is as an instrumental end used to achieve the ultimate goal or *telos* that is unique to human beings. Aristotle concluded that the human *telos* is happiness. "Now such a thing as happiness, above all else, is held to be; for this we choose always for itself and never for the sake of something else..."[10] For Aristotle, happiness is an activity of the soul resulting from living a good life in conformity with excellence, in other words leading a life that is good for a human being. Aristotle leaves open the question of what the good life is, because happiness varies from person to person. Each person works out the content of the good life.[11] It must be added that Aristotle recognized that, although the good life is essentially an activity of the soul, it cannot exist without the support of lesser goods that are external to the soul. "Yet evidently ... it needs the external goods as well; for it is impossible, or not easy, to do noble acts without the proper equipment."[12]

Two other considerations are important in order to have a general idea of Aristotle's thought, because they are the background of MacIntyre's application of Aristotelian philosophy to the modern world. The first is that the *polis*, or society, is essential for acquiring virtue. For Aristotle, there can be no life of virtue outside society, because man is essentially a social being. For him, a human being develops properly only within the community.[13] Virtuous persons consider their well-being to include that of others, not because each can benefit individually from what the others contribute, as would be assumed in an individualistic society, but because together they work out the common good, sharing the resources available to build the good life. (90)

The second consideration is the role of practical reason in the good life. Practical reason is fundamental in the virtuous life because of its function in acquiring virtue. It not only decides how to act, but before acting, practical reason recognizes that action is, in fact, necessary. This ability to judge requires a correct perception of the situation and its moral features. This is the task of practical reason. It is the bridge that links intellectual assessment of a given situation with the decision of what action should take place. "It is clear, then, from what has been said," says Aristotle, "that it is not possible to be good in the strict sense without practical wisdom, nor practically wise without moral excellence." (190-91)

Consequences of the Enlightenment Project

MacIntyre maintains that contemporary post-Enlightenment societies are in a state of disarray partly because they no longer understand the Aristotelian concept of teleology. If life is not directed toward an end and if it is not lived as an effort to achieve that end, the events that make up an individual life are directed toward nothing more transcendent than their own development. MacIntyre laments this dramatic consequence of the enlightenment project as its most serious outcome.

The tendency to live a compartmentalized life, so unlike the past, is one of the most salient traits of post-enlightenment societies. This way of living contributes to the feeling of separation and isolation commonly experienced on the personal and societal levels. Each "piece" of life requires the individual to behave in a way determined by the particular momentary role. "Modernity partitions each human life into a variety of segments, each with its own norms and modes of behavior ... [I]t is the distinctiveness of each and not the unity of the life of the individual who passes through those parts in terms of which we are taught to think and feel."(AV, 203) Many times the conduct specific to each role cannot be transferred successfully to other settings within the life of the same person.

This non-transferability can seem at first glance to be a logical consequence of the fact that one and the same behavior is not appropriate in all situations. This is not what MacIntyre means, however. The fact that conduct cannot be transferred from one context to another is not simply a matter of its being appropriate or inappropriate. The problem, says MacIntyre, is not simply that one does not, in fact, treat one's employees in the same way that one treats one's children. The behavior encouraged by any given situation will, of course, differ from behavior appropriate in a different circumstance. The modern understanding of non-transferability is not so transparent, however. Today the differences lie not only in conduce but also in the fact that the particular moral expectations each situation presents also change.

At the health club many married persons feel free to have "health club" friendships that are an acceptable part of the role of yuppie, but may not be particularly acceptable in the role of wife and mother. An individual may see nothing wrong with dishonest behavior within the corporate world, while at the same time he or she would never consider similar behavior commendable while parenting young children.

When a society nurtures this type of intimate internal division, some people inevitably put a series of contradictory moral behaviors into practice without sensing any contradiction at all. This way of living makes it difficult to see one's life as a unified whole that can pull potentially independent and conflicting roles together, providing a core identity that can be taken into any environment. Without this larger picture of life as a whole directed toward a transcendent goal, people do not try to fit particular events into a larger picture that directs them as persons towards one end. MacIntyre comments:

> That particular actions derive their character as parts of larger wholes
> is a point of view alien to our dominant ways of thinking and yet one
> which is necessary at least to consider if we are to begin to under-
> stand how a life may be more than a sequence of individual actions
> and episodes.(AV, 203)

What is more, another type of division also accompanies this fragmentation of life. This is not the fragmentation of life's activities into isolated segments, but rather a fragmentation of the understanding of the self. MacIntyre calls it the "liquidation of the self ... the emergence of the characteristically modern conceptions of selfhood."(AV, 191) It is understandable and almost inevitable that a person who lives life as a succession of unrelated activities will either consciously or unconsciously conclude that personal identity also boils down to a series of "identities": me as daughter, me as girlfriend, me as professional, etc.

The modern conception of the self no longer provides a sense of inner unity and direction. When what he does determines an individual's self-identity, he adapts to the exigencies of the roles that he assumes and ultimately understands himself only in terms of the activities in which he engages. As a result, he can come to think of himself almost as a series of selves, each with its singular identity and unique way of acting. The one element of life that ought to remain stable, the self, has been broken into as many pieces as different types of activities.

This modern mentality is far from the classical understanding of the self as the source of personal identity enriched by the various experiences that life provides, all the while remaining the same. MacIntyre calls this classical understanding the narrative sense of life, in which individuals write their life stories within the unity that the self provides. (AV, 191) The modern individual cannot begin to see life as a narrative story waiting to be written because the unity that constitutes the narrative life is incomprehensible.

The disintegration of life into individuated roles and the self into fragmented pieces has repercussions at the societal level as well at the personal level. Since post-enlightenment individuals see themselves as isolated pieces with no important ties to those whose lives coincide with theirs, they no longer have a deep sense of membership in society. They can even fail to acknowledge rights and corresponding obligations towards others who live with them in the same society. As opposed to the understanding of self of classical philosophy, the modern self is no longer subjectively embedded within a social and historical framework, even though the individual always works within such a context. The modern self is subjectively "detached" from the classical concept of community envisioned as the sum of its members.

Thus, the members of modern societies no longer see themselves living together in a common community. They think of themselves as citizens who are autonomous individuals. The traditional basis of society, a citizenry that understands their duties toward the common good, no longer exists. Rather than looking after the common good, modern citizens tend to look after their individual rights. "From the standpoint of individualism I am what I myself choose to be. I can always, if I wish to, put in question what are taken to be the merely contingent social features of my existence."(191) The entire notion of virtue has been seriously threatened by this fragmentation of the self and of society, and MacIntyre addresses himself to this threat at great length.

> The liquidation of the self into a set of demarcated role playing allows no scope for the exercise of dispositions which could genuinely be accounted virtue in any sense remotely Aristotelian, for a virtue is not a disposition that makes for success only in some one particular type of situation. (AV, 203)

Virtue is a generalized disposition of the soul. Only the person who thinks of himself as a whole can understand that good habits belong to the person, not to the circumstance. Virtues are good habits taken into many situations rather than behavior tailored to a specific setting.

To compensate for the loss of personal, subjective continuity, essential for personal virtue to flourish, modern society has replaced virtue with an emphasis on skills. By nature skills are designed for and restricted to specific circumstances and needs —they are not cultivated for any environment. The effort to transfer skills honed for one specific purpose to other arenas of action is likely to be less than satisfactory. A skillful executive, for example, who can persuade other board members to do what he wants because of the power and prestige he has within a company, may be at a loss in personal relationships, where power and professional prestige should not be the basis of persuasion.

Virtue, as opposed to skill, is at the disposition of diversity and cannot be defined by a single kind of behavior or situation. Life conceived of as a whole, made of a variety of experiences, uses diversity precisely to create unity. Influence based on power is restricted to the setting in which the individual possesses power, but influence based on friendship is applicable to many situations. "[T]he unity of virtue in someone's life is intelligible only as a characteristic of a unitary life, a life that can be conceived of and evaluated as a whole."(AV, 203)

MacIntyre's Response: The Narrative Life

As mentioned above, MacIntyre asserts that the moral confusion found in modern societies is caused by liberal rejection of the teleological meaning of life and the lack of unity characteristic of the modern world. He espouses the concept of narrative as the way to restore unity both to individuals and to society. In *After Virtue* he asks:

> In what does the unity of an individual life consist? The answer is that its unity is the unity of a narrative embodied in a single life. To ask "What is the good for me?" is to question how I might best live out that unity and bring it to completion. To ask 'What is the good for man?' is to ask what all answers to the former question must have in common. (AV, 203-5)

For MacIntyre, the solution to modern fragmentation lies in restoring narrative meaning to life. Using the narrative story to explain his idea, he says that all of the adventures of a narrative story take on meaning because of the part they play in directing the whole story to its fulfillment. Even though a given adventure may not draw the protagonist closer to what is sought, the incident itself is understood within the context of the more global plot. In a similar way, the narrative life gathers together the various elements that constitute human life and imposes a unity on the diversity that, when experienced outside the narrative framework, becomes a series of isolated incidents.

The essential characteristics of a life lived as a narrative story are continuity of meaning, continuity through time, and continuity in purpose. As opposed to a life lived as a series of events whose main characters are the events themselves, the narrative life has the self as its protagonist. The narrative self can maintain its identity throughout life and within each role it plays precisely because it is not defined by the concrete activities that it undertakes. MacIntyre terms this type of life a life project or "narrative quest."

Virtue can take on meaning only within a life conceived of as a narrative quest. When lived as a quest, life is the pursuit of something. Virtuous dispositions of the soul enable the individual to stick with the search despite setbacks, disappointments, and temptations to give up the quest. Virtue allows the individual to maintain the struggle until completion. What is it that the quest seeks? In concretizing the quest for the good life, MacIntyre divides it into three aspects: the quest for the good determined by the participation in a practice, the personal quest of each individual for the good life, and the common quest for the good life by members of society.

Virtue is essential in all these aspects. In his essay "A Partial Response to My Critics," MacIntyre writes, "On my view no quality is to be accounted a virtue except in respect of its being such as to enable the achievement of three distinct kinds of goods: those internal to practices, those which are the goods of an individual life, and those which are the goods of community."[14] Within practices, a certain level of virtuous behavior is demanded of those who want to be successful. Thus, a child who wants to be a good student must acquire the virtues that will permit success in school and a fisherman must acquire the virtues that will help him to be a good fisherman.

In the personal search for the good life, virtue is indispensable because it assures orientation toward the final goal. The narrative life is deeply social and, as a result, the individual in isolation never achieves virtue. The particular historical and social circumstances of each person's life are also the beginning point for growth in virtue. The individual quest for the good life and participation in practices take place within society, thus linking the individual good to the common quest of the good by all members of society; as Aristotle asserted, man is essentially a social being.[15]

Chapter 2
Practices and Traditions

MacIntyre insists that virtue can be acquired only within a lifestyle that is based on a specific understanding of human nature, the self, society, and education. He has developed two concepts - *practices* and *traditions* – that foster the correct understanding of these notions and that therefore foster growth in virtue. Practices and traditions have specific and complementary roles in individual lives and in the life of society. MacIntyre describes practices in this way:

> Any coherent and complex form of socially established cooperative human activity through which goods internal to that form of activity are realized in the course of trying to achieve those standards of excellence which are appropriate to, and partially definitive of, that form of activity, with the result that human powers to achieve excellence, and human conceptions of the ends and good involved, are systematically extended [1]

Practices

MacIntyre says that practices are a universal feature of all cultures even though the society in which they occur may not recognize them. Life unfolds and flourishes within practices and they form the heart of his discussion of the narrative life of virtue. The activity that takes place within a practice must be coherent, complex, cooperative and, in keeping with the social nature of virtue development, involving more than one person. (Further on we will use the concept of teamwork to illustrate this idea) Those involved in a concrete practice accept its social structure and find strength in the interdependence necessary to complete the task. This acceptance of their interdependence shows that participants understand that each one's good is linked with and somehow dependent upon, the good of the entire group. This is why MacIntyre affirms that activities involving only one person cannot be defined as practices. Playing solitaire, for example, may help to develop certain skills, but by nature it is an activity that one person can perform without the help of others, therefore falling outside the definition of a practice.

A practice involves more than simply cooperative social activity, however. The persons involved must also be able to acquire whatever goods are internal to the practice. In addition, there are two goods internal to all practices- perfection in performing the activity itself and the participants' growth in skills and excellence. MacIntyre describes the internal goods of practices, or crafts, in this way:

> The aim internal to ... crafts, when they are in good order, is never
> only to catch fish or to produce milk ... It is to do so in a manner con-
> sonant with the excellences of the craft, so that not only is there a
> good product, but the craftsperson is perfected through and in her or
> his activity.[2]

Farming's internal goods include milk, vegetables, etc., but they also include the virtue acquired by the workers who take care of the cows and the
fields in the best way possible together, making theirs a good farm and meeting
the standards of excellence that good farming requires.

The example of farming is good because it exemplifies one essential characteristic of all practices: the need to work together. A good farmhand will grow in
virtue personally, but not in isolation. His efforts to work well also contribute to
the other workers' growth in virtue. When each worker is an encouraging example, the overall atmosphere within the practice (farm) will encourage everyone
to strive toward the goal of excellence, making the farm itself efficient as a
whole. Thus, the good of each individual is also part of the good of the whole
community.

MacIntyre also insists that only experienced participants in a given practice
can recognize the goods internal to it. Those who have experience farming and
who have the knowledge of what constitutes the good life as a farmer can understand the internal goods of farming. Those without farming experience cannot
fully understand or appreciate farming's internal goods unless they are willing to
become initiated into it by learning how to farm. In any case, one cannot acquire
virtue and a life of virtue simply by living within a practice. Virtue is acquired
through the effort to meet the standards of excellence that define the activity and
that are appropriate to it. Working in and of itself does not guarantee the acquisition of a practice's internal goods; one must work well.

Meeting a practice's standards of excellence has two stages: accepting the
authority of the standards specific to the practice and obeying the rules that
guarantee excellence and secondly, subjecting attitudes, choices, and preferences to the standards that define the practice. This becomes clear if we consider
the lengths to which a basketball player will go to be considered an excellent
team player. If he wants to be a good player, an aspiring National Basketball
Association team member will work to meet the standards of the National Basketball Association (NBA). He will do this independent of his personal opinion
about them because he knows that it is by trying to meet those standards that he
will play good basketball.

In addition, because of the NBA's standards, our aspiring basketball player
is able to judge whether he, at this moment, is a good player or a mediocre one
who needs to practice more. Thus, by accepting the authority of the standards of
good basketball playing, the player strives for a goal and cultivates an appreciation of the nature of good playing. The NBA standards of excellence teach basketball players how to distinguish between good and bad playing at the same
time that they give the individual an ability to assess his own performance.

Personal relationships and mutual interdependence must also exist within a practice. MacIntyre highlights the importance of truthfulness, justice, and courage in developing relationships within a practice. (AV, 177)

Justice is essential so that favoritism does not overshadow personal relationships and so that one can know who deserves what when goods must be distributed. If justice were missing in a relationship between two members of a practice, it would harm not only that relationship but also other relationships within the practice, by a wrongful distribution of resources. Without the virtue of justice, the joint pursuit of the good is more difficult.

Once again, basketball teams are a good example to illustrate this point. Take the case in which player A and player B are the team's best players. They work well together and consistently pass the ball to each other. The consequences of the exclusive nature of this relationship can have serious repercussions on the rest of the team. Even though the combination of these two players may mean that they win the game, there is more to the proper functioning of a team (practice) than winning (the end product).

The other team members are affected because they are unable to perform the roles for which they have been trained and they are denied the opportunity of working together to create an excellent basketball team. In this example the team has effectively been reduced to showcasing the two star players.

The team spirit that encourages each member of the team to work for the good of all is jeopardized and, as a result, the players no longer function as a team. The team (or practice) has, in effect, been dissolved - it is no longer an activity in which there is interdependence, shared activity, and a generalized common striving to meet the standards of excellence required by the practice: the virtue of justice is absent from relationships among the team players.

Truthfulness and courage affect the proper functioning of the practice in similar ways. When the members of a practice are not truthful, trust becomes difficult, cooperation diminishes, and both individual and group efforts to live virtue are put at risk. Courage is also essential if members of a practice are interdependent and look out for one another's good. Each virtue plays a key role in making the common pursuit of the good by a cooperative group possible. (AV, 178-9)

Relationships within a practice extend beyond its current members. They include in some way those pervious members considered important historical figures within the practice or those whose efforts have made the practice what it is today. Practices have a history; today's standards of excellence are the result of growth in the past. In other words, standards of excellence evolve as the practice and the new skills that perfect it develop and as the conceptions of the goals and goods characteristic of the practice are modified over time.

MacIntyre says "to enter into a practice is to enter into a relationship not only with its contemporary practitioners, but also with those who have preceded us in the practice, particularly those whose achievements extended the reach of the practice to its present point."(AV, 179)

We can see this clearly in the history of basketball. It is easy to recognize modifications in the NBA's standards of excellence as well as modified internal goods such as the new plays, new elements of team work, and modified rules of the game.

> What is distinctive of a practice is in part the way in which concep-
> tions of the relevant goods and ends which technical skills serve ...
> are transformed and enriched by these extensions of human powers
> and by that regard for its own internal goods which are partially de-
> finitive of each particular practice or type of practice. (AV, 181)

The kinds of activities considered practices are many and quite diverse. MacIntyre considers the arts, sciences, making and sustaining family life, games, crafts, certain professions such as medicine, teaching, and social work, all to be practices.(AV, 180) He also argues that as individuals seek the good, they move simultaneously within many practices, each with its own goods. At the same time, each person has a personal good toward which his or her life is directed, and he or she must know which personal goods are being attained by participating in each practice. Life has a single purpose, and participation in practices must lead toward that single goal. Thus, it becomes necessary to priori-tize the goods within each practice, giving them an order of importance in rela-tionship to each other, in relationship to the goods of the other practices, and finally in relationship to the goods essential to the individual's life project. When a person asks the question "What is my good?" the answer must include finding the right place for each good in relation to other goods and to the overall good. Other members of the community can help because the ordering of goods within an individual's life is inseparable from ordering goods in achieving the common good. (AV, 180, 175)

MacIntyre also makes a distinction between goods internal to practices and goods external to them. An external good can be acquired through the exercise of the practice, but it could also be obtained by the exercise of any number of practices. External goods are true and necessary goods, but they can nullify the pursuit of virtue if sought exclusively within one practice. (PR, 288) Fame, eco-nomic remuneration, and power are external goods that can be acquired through any number of practices and are not considered goods internal to any one prac-tice. MacIntyre argues strongly that a practice will flourish and be the setting for a life of virtue only if it is performed exclusively to acquire its proper internal goods, the excellence, and the sense of community that animate a well-ordered practice. He holds that a practice carried out exclusively to obtain external goods can be easily corrupted. Corruption is less likely to take place in a practice whose goal is excellence rather than the extrinsic goods that result from it.

External goods are important because most practices could not exist if they did not bring some financial remuneration to their participants. MacIntyre places practices within *institutions*, which assume the burden of seeking external goods necessary for the sustenance of the practices. Hospitals and doctors' offices are institutions, MacIntyre says, within which the practice of medicine takes place; schools and universities are the institutions within which the practices of teach-ing and learning take place. MacIntyre explains their relationship in this way:

Practices must not be confused with institutions. Chess, physics and medicine are practices; chess clubs, laboratories, universities and hospitals are institutions. Institutions are characteristically and necessarily concerned with what I have called external goods. They are involved in acquiring money and other material goods; they are structured in terms of power and status, and they distribute money, power and status as rewards. Nor could they do otherwise if they are to sustain not only themselves, but also the practices of which they are the bearers. For no practices can survive for any length of time unsustained by institutions. Indeed so intimate is the relationship of practices to institutions... that the cooperative care for common goods of the practice is always vulnerable to the competitiveness of the institution. In this context the essential function of the virtues is clear. Without them, without justice, courage, and truthfulness, practices could not resist the corrupting power of institutions. (PR, 11)

Thus, the setting necessary for a flourishing human life is not an individual search for the good life, but rather a mutually cooperative work in pursuit of goods that will contribute to the individual's good life and to the good of all the members of the practice. The participants work together and share among themselves the benefits derived from work well-done in community.

This brings the discussion of practices into its wider context, that of the *traditions,* without which practices could not survive.

Traditions

Living the Aristotelian good life means living in a community with a spirit of interdependence and a shared understanding of the common good. MacIntyre writes:

A living tradition then is a historically extended, socially embodied argument and an argument precisely in part about the goods which constitute the tradition. Within a tradition the pursuit of goods extends through generations, sometimes through many generations. (AV, 181)

In his book *Habits of the Heart*, Robert Bellah describes the importance of historical tradition: Communities have a history, and in an important sense they are constituted by their past. A community is involved in retelling its story or narrative. In doing so, it offers examples of the men and women who have embodied and exemplified the meaning of the community. The men and women who came before are an important part of the community's tradition. Tradition provides the framework within which the general human good is concretized for each person and within which each member discovers the individual good.[3]

Tradition not only gives the individual a sense of belonging, it also converts that person into what MacIntyre calls a "bearer of tradition." (AV, 207) He argues that, contrary to what liberal philosophy holds, no one can be an autonomous self. No one, he says, is historically independent. The identity of present members of a tradition depends upon links forged in and with the past.

> What I am, therefore, is in key part what I inherit, a specific past that
> is present to some degree in my present. I find myself part of a his-
> tory, and that is generally to say, whether I like it or not, whether I
> recognize it or not, one of the bearers of tradition. I inherit from the
> past of my family, my city, my tribe, my nation, a variety of debts,
> inheritances, rightful expectations and obligations. These constitute
> the given in my life, my moral starting point. This is in part what
> gives my life its own moral particularity. (AV, 214)

In providing the framework for the search for the good, traditions also provide social roles for their members, thus determining what is good for the individual. In an important way, these social roles constitute one's moral starting
point. This is partly because living the good life varies even when everyone has
one and the same conception of the good life. For example, each person is a
member of a specific family living in concrete circumstances that bring with
them economic, social, and psychological limitations. All of these factors combine to define each one's role and to determine the good for the persons who
assume these family roles. Circumstances not only establish each person's role
within the family, but they also determine in part what good each person should
seek. MacIntyre writes,

> The self has to find its moral identity in and through its membership
> in communities such as the family, the neighborhood, the city and the
> tribe ... without those moral particularities to begin from there would
> never be anywhere to begin. (AV, 206)

Not only does tradition help define individual identity, it also sustains practices in two ways: by providing broad guidelines within which practices operate
and by being the occasion of their mutual support based on the tradition that
they share. "The history of a practice in our time," MacIntyre writes, "is generally and characteristically embedded in and made intelligible in terms of the
larger and longer history of the tradition through which the practice in its present
form was conveyed to us." (AV, 204-5) On the one hand, practices depend on
traditions to maintain their identity and orientation. On the other, traditions depend on practices that share the same understanding of the common good for
their existence. Thus, there is an interdependence of practices upon traditions
and traditions upon practices.

In *After Virtue,* MacIntyre argues that liberal societies in which civic participation is between the individual and the state and no longer through the me-
diation of the neighborhood or local community have lost the ability to appreciate the importance of intermediate communities based in practice and human
relations, where learning is transmitted and where we learn to conceive of ourselves as part of an 'us,' rather than an 'I.' Liberal societies as they exist in the
contemporary world cannot sustain the Aristotelian life of virtue because, at
their core, we find only isolation and fragmentation, which hamper the sense of
tradition and community that MacIntyre feels is necessary.

MacIntyre does realize that traditions and practices must be able to survive
within the larger context of liberal societies that do not participate in his concep-

tion of the good. He has no interest in trying to change liberal societies because on his view past attempts have failed. He has chosen to focus his efforts on preserving traditions in small, local communities.

> It is in key part in the lives of families, parishes, schools, clinics, work places, and local neighborhoods and communities that any particular conception of the good achieves recognizable form. (AV, 207)

MacIntyre acknowledges that tradition-based communities do exist within liberal societies, but, he says, they exist on the outskirts, marginalized by a liberal context that tolerates them. He argues, however, that this is the only way these traditions can survive. In fact, he recommends that small communities isolate themselves from contact with more global forms of government in an effort to remain intact. "On occasion the maintenance and defense of local forms of community may demand, of course, some type of ad hoc participation in global political systems. But this participation ought to remain limited to very precise situations." (207)

MacIntyre's political interest lies only in these small communities. "What should our political activity be? This is my answer: the construction and promotion on the local level of forms of community and social relations based on the activity of a praxis."[4] He insists on the importance of households, neighborhoods, and schools because it is possible to build a spirit of cooperative work towards a common goal within each of them. These small communities have ties with similar communities, each having its own particular structure of authority and its own education regarding the particular goods it pursues. As such, all of these communities are places in which virtue can be lived and taught. "I am interested," he continues, "exclusively in those political forms in which and through which the life of virtue can be given a social identity and in which mutual responsibility can be re-established." [5]

MacIntyre says that the only people who will be interested in his ideas about virtue and the virtuous life are those who see their life's work in terms of *craft*.

> Realistically, I hope to be heard exclusively by those people whose activities are considered marginal by those who occupy positions of power in contemporary societies. Small farmers, teachers who refuse to be made-over into bureaucrats, everyone who conserves the ideal of a craft in their manual and intellectual work; members of cooperatives dedicated to eradicating hunger or housing the homeless; these people are the ideal readers of my works ... I would have to add [to this list] some small businessmen, some professors, and certain types of doctors.[6]

Chapter 3
Educating for Good Character

What is Education?

For MacIntyre, the main goal of education is to enable students to act in accord with the *télos* of the good life, becoming virtuous persons within the setting of their inherited traditions. Education is crucial in maintaining and keeping practices and traditions alive because it fosters the development of virtue, an awareness of the narrative nature of life, and the continuity necessary to live the narrative life.

In keeping with Aristotelian educational theory, MacIntyre asserts that the pupil, through instruction and character formation, is the protagonist of the educational process, assuming an increasingly dominant role in his or her own education.[1] As students progress and grow older, they gradually internalize underlying principles until they come to the stage in which teachers and other adults no longer need to be the primary motivators in their learning; students will have acquired the dispositions that allow them to become life-long learners, the ideal members of any tradition and community. According to MacIntyre, the purpose of the educational process is the cultivation of stable inner dispositions (virtues) that allow the individual, guided by his or her own sound judgment, to lead a life directed toward the good. Education is essentially educating the practical intellect, whose chief virtue is sound judgment.

MacIntyre also maintains that education is essential if students are to remain faithful to the narratives, traditions, and practices into which they were born and within which they are being educated. Education ensures continuity within traditions and the historical continuity of traditions themselves. MacIntyre does not advocate a blind attachment to either practice or tradition, however. He is of the view that goods within traditions can and do change over time and he advocates a critical spirit capable of taking the best and incorporating it into a personal quest for the good.

It is easy to understand why education in good character is at the heart of MacIntyre's notion of education. Education is not so much a matter of the information a student may receive as it is learning how to live well. Curricular reform will not do much to improve education, he says, because it is the philosophy and goals upon which the curriculum is based that will ultimately prove to be its success or its failure.(TV, 625) Growth in virtue, when properly carried out, ensures a sound intellectual education as well. Furthermore, the basic goals of education in general and character education are one and the same, the distinction being that, whereas a theory of education will state that virtue education is essential, character education teaches the "how" of growth in virtue.

Education in Good Character

Student motivation in moral growth is very important. Initially, MacIntyre holds, students do the good for their personal satisfaction or because they want to please the adults, mainly their parents and teachers, who provide their security.[2] He says that children realize very quickly that specific types of behavior please their mothers, teachers, etc., and they frequently behave well not because a specific behavior is good, but rather to please the adults who are important to them. MacIntyre argues that one sign of moral maturity is the transition from pleasing others to valuing good precisely because it is good.

MacIntyre also warns, however, that unless students are able to make the transition from personal satisfaction and a desire to please to seeking good and living virtue as a means to acquiring the good, they will not develop the correct understanding of virtue. (HSV, 8) Even though a child may perform actions that conform to the definition of virtuous action, actions that in themselves are identical to the actions of a virtuous person, in reality the student will not be acting virtuously. As a result, when transitioning to the next stage of in moral growth, inferring ways to live a specific virtue in a variety of circumstances, the student will almost inevitably come to wrong conclusions.

MacIntyre challenges teachers and parents to discover ways to transform students' motivation for doing good because of the danger of growing older without developing a more autonomous motivation for acting in a specific way. The older student who continues to act mainly to please teachers and parents does not seek the good in and of itself. When pleasing parents and teachers remains the main motivation for striving for good grades, a student may think that stealing a copy of a final exam or lying would be the best action to take. Older students still trying to please will have learned erroneously that virtue is causing others, especially those adults upon whom they depend, to be pleased with them. They will not have learned that virtue is the disposition that makes doing good easier in general, whether or not it pleases others. Later in life these same students may expand this mistaken idea and think that virtue, or at least the right thing to do, is to please anyone who provides you with a secure social environment.

If older students' main motivation for doing good is to please others, they will think of vice in the same way that they think of virtue; a vice will become anything that causes pain either to themselves or to others. Their false understanding of both virtue and vice will be based on producing pleasure and avoiding pain rather than understanding the relation between their télos and the need of living in a way that will permit them to attain it. (HSV, 10) It is incumbent upon teachers to discover ways to help students make the transition from satisfying the self or others to seeking the good for its own sake. It is precisely here, unfortunately, that MacIntyre falls silent. He does not offer any suggestions, possibly because, to a certain extent, there are no standard techniques in a task as personal as this, but mainly, it might be argued, because it is beyond the scope of MacIntyre's interest as a philosopher.

Sound Judgment

Still, MacIntyre does provide a description of the process that a virtuous person will follow in deciding what action is appropriate in a given situation. Students who have learned to perform good acts because they want to do the good will be motivated primarily, he says, by the knowledge and love of the télos, and not principally because of the pleasure that may be the result of an action. This is the reason why, for example, older students will frequently exhibit constancy in peer tutoring despite homework loads, the weather, or how they feel. Younger students, when motivated by good feelings or the admiration of the children they help, cannot sustain a commitment when they do not feel like tutoring or when they have a headache. Part of moral maturity is the realization that pain and pleasure do not provide the proper grounding for virtue, especially social virtue. Older students will have learned that what pleases or pains a virtuous person is not necessarily what pleases or pains an immature person. (HSV, 13)

MacIntyre argues that character education can be divided into two stages that reflect the manner in which young people grow in virtue. In the first stage, the child acknowledges the teacher's authority in moral issues, coinciding with the innate desire young children have to please. MacIntyre recommends reading as a basic tool at this stage. He recommends epic, heroic, and Biblical literature because of the vivid and attractive pictures they provide of persons who live virtue in pursuit of the good. Because of the impact that reading has on children, MacIntyre also suggests some type of censorship, something, he says, done naturally by those adults whose job it is to guide the growth of the young. (HSV, 16, 15)

It is during this early period that children acquire the proper dispositions for virtue and learn to act virtuously by example, without complex explanations. The heroes of the stories that they read can serve as role models for the young without requiring inappropriate abstract considerations. MacIntyre's recommended readings are an integral part of learning virtue by example, guiding the passions and behavior long before children are able to study virtue effectively in theory.

During this initial stage, students become grounded in a specific virtue system, they acquire a trust of authority, and they acquire the appropriate character virtues. Stage two takes children one step further. In the second stage students begin training in sound moral judgment. (HSV, 16) At this point, MacIntyre argues that the main objective is education in sound judgment, the most essential element of all character education. He warns that this training is inappropriate for the very young because it presupposes some experience in the moral life, and the very young do not usually have a wide enough range of experience. Until students have some experience in following rules and in controlling their emotions, they cannot be expected to derive appropriate conclusions from advanced character education, nor do they have the foundation upon which sound judgment is based.

In order to develop sound judgment, students first learn to conceptualize and classify. These capacities become very important when students apply universal concepts to concrete situations. If they cannot conceptualize and classify, they will not be able to make an accurate description of the very situation that is the subject of moral consideration. When students cannot describe a concrete circumstance accurately, they will not know which general rule to apply, nor will they be able to generalize from the particulars of the situation. The development of the ability to conceptualize and classify, then, is the first step of the second stage of MacIntyre's character education. (HSV, 14)

Once students have acquired these two skills, they are ready for the introduction of systemic controversies between differing moral groups given from the viewpoint of their own moral system. In this way, students learn about the larger moral and social context of which they are a part and the important moral issues that shape the politics and culture of their country. At the same time they have already begun to internalize the theoretical structure and to appreciate the support that their own moral system supplies. (14)

The development of sound judgment is the key to being able to live a narrative life and the explanation for the narrative life's freedom from overdependence upon rules and regulations. As students grow older they use their sound judgment when deciding which practices to take up and which virtues they need. (15)

Sound judgment functions in two ways when choosing which practices to become involved in: it acts as the student's cultural memory and as a philosophic imagination. When acting as cultural memory, sound judgment brings to mind the goods that the students have inherited from their tradition. When acting as philosophic imagination, sound judgment personalizes the objective excellences students find in their tradition, fitting these goods and excellences into their own life project in a creative and original way. (TV, 632)

Character education that fosters sound judgment enables students to transcend the boundaries of what they have strictly inherited. They can now give new and updated interpretations to the tradition that they have inherited that will enrich it for present needs and that will make it a more apt base for future development. In MacIntyre's opinion, the key to all educational success and the success of character education in particular, is uniting the objective dimension of tradition to the subjective situation of the person, thereby personalizing the tradition's *télos*. (AV, 141)

The education that MacIntyre thinks is appropriate and necessary for living well in the modern world is one that cultivates virtue. It stresses personal growth in virtue, especially sound judgment. Thus individuals can, with a sense of belonging, participate in and critically evaluate the traditions they inherit from the local community. They can lead lives that have direction and purpose both as individuals and as a community.

MacIntyre and Dewey

MacIntyre and Dewey forward conceptions of education that they think respond to the needs of the modern world and of contemporary American society and one may be struck by their similarities. The two men consider character education the most important part of the educational process; they both think that the individual is intimately linked to society, unable to develop properly outside of a social framework. When speaking of social progress, Dewey and MacIntyre both cite the need of critical thinking and evaluation and they both think that members of society who have these skills are a society's most important members.

Despite their common concerns, however, their views of education differ radically. One could ask why and the answer would be straightforward: it is the consequence of differing conceptions of the human person, the nature of society, the relationship between person and society, the role of education in society, and the purpose and focus of character education in relation to the person and in relation to society.

In the first section of this book we discussed the need to enunciate the philosophical tradition within which a given character education is framed, in order to determine which type of character education is best for contemporary American society. Indeed, from the discussions of Dewey and MacIntyre it is clear that philosophical foundations are decisive in determining the nature and implementation of character education. Nevertheless, just as the modern world is characterized by complexity, implementing character education in today's world is also complex.

It is important to approach this issue with an open mind, and so, in the final section of this study, contributions from both Dewey and MacIntyre are used in reflecting on and in making recommendations for the ongoing debate over the role and focus of character education within American society.

PART IV
A NEW VISION

Person, Education & Society

The future of the American society hinges largely on whether or not we educate in the correct way about important issues and whether or not our young people develop into good people. Educational research, and especially research into character and its development, should have pride of place in our universities. The study of the most effective ways to promote good character is of utmost importance, for it is increasingly evident that the focus given to character education directs the development of young personalities and young citizens.

This chapter will examine character education in schools. As both Dewey and MacIntyre remind us, however, character education never simply happens; it is couched within the framework of a specific educational philosophy either implicitly or explicitly, and derives its style and content from this broader context.

Person, Education & Society

Dewey and MacIntyre understand that development of good character is essential to American education. In fact, both men consider it to be *the* most important aspect of education. At the same time, the bench marks of character growth suggested could not be more polarized. Dewey's idea of education as growth, for example, is far removed from MacIntyre's concept of education in virtue. This discussion begins by trying to uncover the cause of these differences. Dewey and MacIntyre understand that character education is necessary because of its purpose, and its purpose is what separates the two.

For Dewey, pupils are essentially nascent members of a liberal democratic society who need to learn how to fulfill the social roles that await them. Within his framework, the purpose of education is to inculcate the qualities necessary for successful participation in a democracy, guiding students from an early age by means of democratic experiences in the school setting. Character education teaches pupils to be good democratic citizens.[1]

MacIntyre views pupils as persons writing the narrative story of their lives. This process includes growing in the virtues that will help students to face the demands that life will make of them. MacIntyre envisions character education taking place within the practices and traditions into which students have been born and educated. While their inherited traditions support them, however, children also learn how to improve upon them. (AV, 203) Dewey is committed to a concept of democracy that demands committed citizens capable of shouldering the weight of society's ever-changing direction. For him, inherited traditions have value only as the basis for new responses to situations requiring democratic reconstruction. Education teaches students that they must reconstruct society, and character education teaches them how to do this.[2]

In contrast, MacIntyre argues that the liberal democracy Dewey wants to perpetuate is the greatest of all obstacles to a good education. (AP, 143) In MacIntyre's scheme, character education enables pupils to identify with and to enrich the traditions of their local communities, giving them a sense of belonging and personal identity. He argues that one ought to seek out and live in these small communities, where traditions and practices can exist independent of global politics. (AV, 207)

The ideas forwarded in this final section use MacIntyre's definition of student and the purposes of character education that he suggests. This is the virtue character education model that seconds MacIntyre's emphasis on the practices and traditions discussed in Part III, turning the school's hidden curriculum into a powerful tool for education in virtue.

MacIntyre's instinctive isolationism is not a suitable or necessary response to the challenges of our liberal society. (DV, 92) Those who agree with MacIntyre's critique of liberalism need not feel the need to protect themselves to the point of disengagement from society. They will become the kind of citizens American democracy is looking for, even if currently they may not be the kind of citizens it has. In the long run, children who have experienced a strong local community and a personalized education in virtue will become a liberal democracy's most influential citizens, although perhaps not in a liberal fashion. These citizens could be the basis of the renewal of American society that many leaders desire.

Unfortunately, some contemporary character education projects differ from the models presented by both Dewey and MacIntyre in one fundamental way - they are primarily result-oriented, educating for specific behaviors, rather than educating in principles that can lead to any number of virtuous behaviors.

Much of contemporary character education appears be drifting away from educational philosophy. Numerous contemporary approaches to character education have evolved as a response to social changes rather than from a better understanding of the nature and purpose of education. Strategies vary not from philosophy to philosophy, but rather from classroom to classroom. "Experts tracking the growing interest in character education attribute this trend to public pressure to reduce antisocial student behavior and produce more respectful and responsible citizens," says Roberta McKay in her article "Character Education: A Question of Character."[3] The dominant force in character education today is the public's perception of a decline in morally good behavior. The role of character education seems to be that of filling in the moral holes that have sprung up despite the strategies employed until now. Viewing education and children as the solution to social problems, however, runs the risk of producing persons who are issue- and situation-oriented, rather producing than the virtuous citizens that our society needs.[4]

Although there is every reason to be seriously concerned about moral problems in our society, character education ought to focus on the good of individual children rather than trying to remediate social deficiencies. This does not imply that it should ignore social problems, but rather that character education should not revolve solely around circumstances or issues that jeopardize social stability. When properly focused, character education will promote good citizenship and positive social change precisely because the values children will acquire are good and desirable.

Promoting character education strategies without also knowing the educational philosophy that backs them up is a serious mistake. Character education needs to regain its place within a solid philosophy of education so that it can be, as both Dewey and MacIntyre envisioned, the heart of all education.

Character Education Reformers

Although the above does reflect the current situation to a great degree, some educators and researchers have been studying alternatives. William Damon thinks that we should make schools places where children learn both competence and character: First, schools must become places where all children can find personal relationships that guide them toward shared community standards, where each child is treated as an individual. Second, schools must engage children in activities that foster disciplined understanding. Third, schools must uphold clear standards that lead children to develop good habits and dispositions of character. Damon's mention of "disciplined understanding" and not merely "understanding" suggests the central role that character plays in academic success. (GE, 205)

Thomas Lickona also recognizes the importance of self-discipline. He writes, "Behind the capacity to work is an important quality of character, the ability to delay gratification. … It is this … alone that makes possible serious and consistent learning over long period of time."(EFC, 211-12) Thus, as Damon and Lickona suggest, schools should foster a love of learning. Love of learning places special emphasis on building self-discipline, a prerequisite for academic pursuits and for life in general. Schools are the perfect place to encourage virtues such as a willingness to work hard, thus delaying gratification, a sense of responsibility, respect for truth and knowledge, development of critical and creative thinking, good use of freedom, and a desire to use one's intellect and learning in the pursuit of goodness for oneself and for others. Emphasizing love for learning fosters many virtues as students strive to live up to this ideal.[5]

Respect, the root of many other virtues, is also very important for overall growth in good character. Among other good habits, respect demands cooperation and acceptance of one's peers, in addition to the appropriate deference for authority.

Education involves growth in inner dispositions that aim at personal, social and professional excellence, all-important in a pluralistic society. Since growth in virtue is a life-long endeavor, fostering respect and love of learning underscores education's social character and leads to life-long learning. Schools based on educational principles such as those proposed by MacIntyre and Aristotle can thus fulfill Damon's challenge: "Schools must represent the highest values in society and must expect excellence in intellectual and social comportment from every student."(GE, 25)

In his book *The Rehabilitation of Virtue,* Robert Sandin writes that "the heart of the concept [of virtue] is the notion of excellence, and the meaning of the term [excellence] varies with the nature of the subject characterized. Thus there is an excellence for a whole range of human activities from musical arts to statesmanship."[6] If our public schools used the theoretical framework proposed here (education as growth in virtue plus Damon's three goals) they would have a very solid foundation.

Finally, this framework (a philosophy of education concretized in school-wide goals of love for learning and respect) brings philosophical principals back to character education. With a philosophy to support it, character education can best perform its task.

Chapter 1

School Philosophy and Mission Statements

Creating a Philosophy Statement

When a school plans character education initiatives, it first needs to formulate the philosophy of education that it will use to develop its program. These principles are a written statement of the ideals that motivate all of the activities that take place.

By using its school philosophy statement as the framework for further clarification of its fundamental nature and purpose, the school can formulate a mission statement: its concrete educational goals and character education strategies. The philosophy statement guarantees unity as well as ensuring continuity in the values put into practice in every classroom. The importance of the school philosophy statement cannot be exaggerated. It clarifies the school's values for parents, faculty, and administration and provides a framework for dialogue about the nature and aims of the school's education. Having a concrete philosophy of education helps schools to maintain a unified outlook while encouraging a rich diversity of activities.

> Before education can occur, educational aims must be present. Thus it is essential that those intending to educate know to what end they wish or ought to educate. Only once this is established will they be in a position to search for methods through which their chosen aims could possibly be realized.[1]

The School Mission Statement

Schools want their faculty and staff to make a personal commitment to the school's vision of education and to work to make that vision a reality. The philosophy statement in and of itself does not provide concrete guidance for educational practice, however.

It is meant to provide parameters rather than goals and objectives. Consequently, faculty, staff, students, and parents must also be familiar with the school's mission statement. The mission statement, which translates the theoretical framework of the philosophy statement into concrete educational goals, provides staff and faculty the practical orientation that they need.[2]

Sample Philosophy and Mission Statements

There seem to be few schools in the Untied States that have philosophy statements written along the lines described above. Most of the schools reviewed have statements combining guiding principles and concrete approaches to character education. The Willows Academy, where I have worked for twenty-five years, has articulated two distinct documents – a mission statement and a philosophy statement.

Although the educators who originally crafted these documents do not agree with my thesis that the philosophy statement should precede the mission statement in much the same way as the end-in-view must precede the means to that end, I have used excerpts from both of these documents because The Willows has tried to make a distinction between educational philosophy and educational mission. On my view the concrete examples stated in the philosophy statement are an integral part of a mission statement, explicating the manner in which a school plans to put its educational ideals into practice.

The Willows Academy, Des Plaines, IL
Philosophy Statement:

> At The Willows Academy we believe the greatest gift parents and educators can offer young women is a sense of mission and personal dignity coupled with the skills and knowledge necessary for a fulfilling and meaningful life. The educational experience offered by The Willows Academy emphasizes six guiding principles.
>
> Celebrating Women's Special Gifts - in addition to the well-known and widely documented advantages of single-sex education for girls… we celebrate her gifts and encourage their use in the service of others.
>
> Freedom with Responsibility – opportunities for exercising personal liberty, understanding consequences, and establishing a lifelong basis for decision making in professional and family life.
>
> Academic Excellence – critical thinking, problem solving and cooperative learning…
>
> Character Development – personal advising and mentoring program … Parental collaboration – ensures that each girl reaches her greatest potential…
>
> Encountering God in Daily Life – teachings of the Catholic Church, daily Mass, spiritual guidance.[3]

Mission Statement:

> The Willows Academy is an independent school for young women in grades six to twelve. The Willows provides its students the necessary means to grow in knowledge, virtue and responsibility. The school is committed to providing a college-preparatory academic program of the highest caliber, a moral atmosphere complementary to that of the home and character formation designed to instill lifelong values. The

> Willows Academy is inspired by the teachings of the Catholic Church
> and the spirituality of the Prelature of Opus Dei.[4]

Through its mission statement, The Willows informs its faculty, staff, students and prospective as well as current parents of the basic values of the school – cooperation with parents, college preparatory curriculum, virtue and spiritual growth.

Its philosophy statement mentions concrete goals the school has set for itself and for its students: single-sex education for girls, service to others; good use of personal freedom, understanding that actions have consequences; critical thinking, problem solving, and cooperative learning; a personal advising and mentoring program; daily Mass and spiritual guidance.

More Philosophy Statements

The Benjamin Franklin Elementary School, Meriden CT
Philosophy Statement

> The Benjamin Franklin School has high expectations for all students
> regardless of their race, ethnicity, or economic status. All students
> will be given the opportunity to achieve their intellectual, physical,
> social, and emotional potential through an environment that builds
> self-esteem, encourages mutual respect, and promotes chances to de-
> velop special talents. We want our children to become responsible,
> forward-thinking, and contributing members of society [5]

Educational Principles – The PARED Schools in Australia

> Under the rubric of *educational principles*, this organization de-
> scribes both its philosophy of education and its mission.
> The Schools' personalized system of education is based on a number
> of principles:
> The education of children is primarily the responsibility of parents
> and is determined to a great extent by the personal example of the
> parents themselves.
> The student benefits most when there is harmony between the two
> major learning environments of home and school; therefore, parents
> and teachers should try to grow in the qualities they wish the students
> to acquire.
> Teachers are vital partners with parents in a common endeavor. The
> basis of this partnership is a loyal and mutual understanding of each
> other's complementary roles.
> Parents and teachers need ongoing professional formation as educa-
> tors who are striving for excellence.
> The student's behaviour should be the consequence of personal con-
> victions, acquired in a climate that balances discipline and freedom as
> the basis for an authentic sense of responsibility.[6]

More Mission Statements

The following are excerpts taken from school mission statements that also emphasize the importance of character education. Each school articulates this commitment in its own way and highlights aspects of character pertinent to its unique educational goals. These schools also tend to combine philosophy statement-type language with their school's mission statement. Were they to distinguish between philosophy of education and mission, these schools could make more powerful statements in both areas.

The Benjamin Franklin Elementary School, Meriden CT –

> The Benjamin Franklin School community is committed to enhancing the lives of children by providing a challenging, supportive and creative environment which fosters self-esteem, responsibility, academic achievement and respect for individual achievement.[7]

Germantown Settlement Charter School, Philadelphia, PA

> Mission Statement: The Germantown Settlement Charter School will help prepare 512 students in grades 5 to 8 for civic leadership through a rigorous academic program that approaches world class standards. Civic leadership, social development and multicultural understanding are also critical goals. The educational program will be based on the Micro Society model, which features learning through simulations of institutions, such as businesses and legislatures, and real-world experiences. Additionally, the school will encourage parental involvement at all levels of the educational program and will develop a strong network of supports for the children and their families.[8]

Montrose School, Natick, MA

> Montrose is an independent college preparatory day school for girls grades 6-12.
> Montrose's mission is to educate the whole person. Built upon the foundation of a rich liberal arts curriculum, personal character formation, and close collaboration with parents, a Montrose education challenges each student to cultivate
> • Intellect and character
> • Leadership and service
> • Faith and reason
> Veritas, Caritas, Libertas emblazoned across the school's shield draw the ideals of a Montrose education into focus. Together with parents Montrose endeavors to help young women pursue the truth in all they do, love God and others selflessly, and use their freedom well.[9]

Freire Charter School, Philadelphia, PA

> *Mission Statement*: Freire Charter School gives young people complementary academic and applied opportunities in a small learning community that is shaped equally by individual goals and democratic ideals, and that provides an inclusive, supportive, respectful, demanding and joyous environment for students, their families, and staff and community partners. The school builds on the insights of educator-philosopher Paolo Freire in connecting students' learning to family,

home, workplace and community. The school will adopt principles of "mindfulness" developed by Harvard psychologist Ellen Langer and will incorporate active learning methods from the work of research-practitioner Eric Rofes. To ensure ongoing dialogue among school, home and mentors, and shared learning activities for students and families, the school will make computer technology and Internet access available to every student and family. Students (and families and staff) will develop personal education plans that take their interests and lifelong learning goals into account. Students graduate with their own well-researched plans that are rooted in rigorous academic learning, systematic service, career and entrepreneurial experiences and reflection.[10]

YouthBuild Charter School, Philadelphia, PA

Mission Statement: The mission of the YouthBuild Philadelphia Charter School is to provide the highest level of opportunities for inner city youth who have not been successful in traditional school settings.[11]

Embers Elementary School, Northfield IL

Embers Elementary is a private, independent school, rooted in the Catholic Faith, serving grades Kindergarten through Fifth. Emphasizing the vocation of the laity, Embers is committed to the pursuit of academic excellence and character formation. Embers works in partnership with parents, who are the primary educators of their children. Embers sees each student as a child of God and a gift from God and helps them to acquire knowledge, develop skills, and practice moral behavior.[12]

Eugenio Maria Dehostos Charter School, Philadelphia, PA

Mission Statement: The mission of the Eugenio Maria DeHostos Community Bilingual Charter School (hereafter referred to as Hostos Charter School) is to promote excellence by providing middle level students a bilingual, bicultural academically enriched curriculum that draws from the social historical experience of Puerto Rico and Puerto Ricans living in the United States. This curriculum will provide all students a clear sense of their cultural identity, a critical approach to the history of Puerto Rico as part of the Americas and Caribbean, and they will develop a strong social change commitment to their community. The school will provide a rigorous curriculum that will fuse high technology with the arts and project-based instruction. We believe that school should be a place that is characterized by respect, critical thinking, democratic classrooms, and the vigorous challenges that are essential to maximize every student's potential. In addition, at the core of the Hostos Charter School is the unity and empowerment of the community, parents, students, teachers, and staff of the schools.[13]

Lincoln Middle School, Meriden, CT

The Mission: Higher order thinking is in the spotlight at Lincoln Middle School, Meriden, Connecticut. The refraction of learning through the prism of the arts is opening opportunities for creative self-expression as well as the mastery of the fundamental core of academic studies. "Learning through the Arts" is the mission of our school. Lincoln's participation as a H.O.T. School© is a significant part of how the arts are infused into the students' daily activities. The disciplines found in the arts curriculum uniquely promote creativity, self-expression, and communication. When students combine these skills and talents with the rest of their academic curriculum we believe they will create interests and learning that they will use the rest of their lives.[14]

Continuity and Change in Character Education

To make sure that virtue education is put into practice, whatever form character education strategies take, a school's commitment to education in virtue should be reflected first of all in the school philosophy statement, next in the school mission statement, and lastly in the character education strategy itself. Once this commitment has been established, any number of strategies can be implemented without betraying the foundation upon which the strategies are based.

The importance of forging explicit links between character education and the philosophy statement becomes apparent when evaluating strategy effectiveness. The school in which I work is an all-girls middle and high school. Our philosophy statement (excerpted above) takes an emphatic stand on the value of single sex education for girls by "celebrating women's special gifts." The fine arts department has concretized this commitment by providing our students with the opportunity to participate in stage productions composed solely of girls. Adolescent girls grow in self-confidence more easily when the subtle social pressures that come with boys are absent. Teenage girls, however, do not necessarily appreciate this opportunity for self-confidence to the same degree that the fine arts department and the school administration do.

To help students and some parents understand the rationale behind the school's commitment to all-girl casts and crews, the administration was able to appeal to the philosophy statement as the guiding document in decisions of this sort. Although some students do not agree with the school's commitment in this issue, they can understand, albeit reluctantly, that the school has a philosophy to uphold, and that the task of the administration and Board of Directors is to carry out the philosophy as best they can. Besides, the girls can participate in their local community theater productions if they so choose.

Coming to that decision, however, was not easy. We knew that the number of good all-female productions is much smaller than the number of good productions composed of men and women. We also realized that our job was made more difficult because of our self-imposed imitations. We asked ourselves whether having coeducational dramatic productions would change the mission statement and whether a change of this type would enhance or derail the school's philosophy.

We had to decide whether a change of this type could unwittingly change the school's orientation. It became obvious very soon that if we rewrote the mission statement to include coeducational activities we would lose the quality that makes our character education unique – its being designed exclusively for girls. The philosophy statement acted as a reminder for us of the fundamental principles upon which the school is based and it helped us keep practice in line with theory.

Chapter 2
Respect & Love of Learning

Character education ought to be one of the most important components of any school's educational package. That is why, in addition to knowing the philosophy that underlies the education that they offer, administrators and teachers first need to determine the focus and style that they want to give to their character education before choosing a specific strategy. After pinpointing the focus for their school, administrators must agree on how to create a favorable climate. After these two steps, a mission statement can be formulated that provides practical orientation for faculty, staff, administration, and parents. Ideas from both John Dewey and Alasdair MacIntyre will be helpful in making these decisions.

The Context for Character Education: The Hidden Curriculum

Dewey and MacIntyre agree that growth is crucial in character development. Although they define growth differently and come to different conclusions regarding its development, Dewey and MacIntyre have some interesting points in common. Both of these thinkers realize that the context within which character grows is not a specific place or activity - it is the totality of a child's school experience. Everything about a school can and does influence a young person's character, especially the school's culture.

MacIntyre's definition of growth revolves around his notion of continuity of personal identity through time and circumstance. This concept is important for educators because it clarifies where and when character education takes place at school. MacIntyre argues that the whole child is the subject of all education. As a result, a young person's character cannot be shaped completely by participating in activities whose sole objective is cognitive knowledge, even cognitive knowledge of character. Everything in which students are involved, MacIntyre says, is an opportunity for them to grow in virtue. Every facet of school life can be, and is, character forming. (AV, 191). Dewey also emphasizes the fact that children's characters are shaped by all of their experiences; character is molded all the time, not only when the child takes part in activities that are intentionally educational. (CTY, 186-7). A school's culture or environment, which penetrates every facet of school life, has been called its *hidden curriculum* because it comprises all of the "personal and social learnings that a student absorbs apart from classroom instruction.[1] The school environment is especially influential, because students do not perceive it to be intentionally educational. Edwin Delattre notes the importance of the hidden curriculum in character education when he writes:

> Even where there is no explicit or didactic mention of good charac-
> ter's fundamental importance, adults and children learn by participa-
> tion in a morally serious home or school... Especially for children,
> who are growing in so many ways, being in such a climate serves
> powerfully to promote the learning of those habits which constitute
> good character... It is truly forged midst the heat and noise and buf-
> feting of daily living.[2]

The basic context of character education in schools then, is the environment of the school as a whole: its classrooms, the hallways, the cafeteria, the
gym, its teachers, the subject matter studied, the non-teaching staff, sports, as-
semblies, relationships of all types, etc. Everything that occurs within and
around the school can be the occasion of character education. William Kilpatrick
writes about the hidden curriculum in this way:

> To the extent that character formation takes place in school, much of
> it is accomplished through the spirit and atmosphere of a school, its
> sports and symbols, its activities and assemblies, its purposes and
> priorities, its codes of conduct and responsibility - most of all through
> its teachers and the quality of their example. Ultimately, character
> education is the responsibility of the school's whole environment.
> That makes character education a very big undertaking but not an
> impossible one. Schools are not the only arena for character educa-
> tion, but schools are a very important arena and are one place to
> start.[3]

The hidden curriculum is the most effective means of character education
that any school has. I have spoken with many parents who, even though academic demands were high, lament having sent their children to a given school
because of the negative influence the school's environment had on their children's attitudes toward authority and the values fostered in their homes.

I have also spoken to parents who are very thankful for the positive environments of other schools because their children have overcome shyness, they
have learned to work hard, and they have dropped the hard rebellious edge that
they had been acquiring. Even children understand the importance a virtue-
friendly environment. Throughout my years of teaching, many older students
have referred to the adaptation process new students go through as "learning our
spirit." They know that our school stands for specific values: hard work, kind-
ness to one another and commitment to school and family, etc. It is a point of
pride for them to participate in a school whose spirit embodies these values.

Respect and Caring

As Dewey and most educators rightly understand, character education is being carried out twenty-four hours a day. Our concern here, however, is with the
six or seven hours of each weekday during which a child's school experience is
the main instrument of this process.

Dewey also points to the significance of hidden curriculum when he writes, "collateral learning in the way of formation of enduring attitudes, of likes and dislikes, may be and often is much more important than the spelling lesson or lesson in geography or history that is learned."[4] How can a school's climate encourage virtue or excellence? Students learn to value excellence when the environment in which they study encourages both love of learning and respect. (EFC, 325)

When a school's climate fosters helpfulness, trust, and mutual concern among peers, faculty, and administration, students learn as they watch the adults around them. A consistently caring and respectful environment is critical if children are to realize that these virtues should be a primary concern for adults. Children need more than quality time from adults, for one cannot care for or respect others episodically. Lickona has said this to say about the importance of an environment of caring:

> We want students to become the kind of people who will do what's right even when they're surrounded by a rotten culture. But forming that sort of character is much easier in a moral environment where being honest, decent, and caring is perceived to be the norm - what everybody simply expects of everybody else. (EFC, 227)

Students are usually willing to do their best if they sense that the teachers and other school personnel are interested in them personally. On the contrary, if students sense that the adults in charge of their school are primarily interested in a smooth-running institution, publishing impressive school statistics or getting the school into the local press, they may not find much motivation for working hard.

It is especially important that teachers and other adults who deal with students on a personal level examine the attitudes that they exhibit toward people and work while in school. When teachers return homework or written assignments with a grade but no encouraging personal comment, they have missed a chance to help students to value excellence. If high school teachers do not compliment school athletes after winning a game, the players will not learn from their teachers' example that mutual concern means thinking of others and looking for the opportunity to show interest and affection.

If the principal finds that she has not said hello to any students after walking down the hall, she has lost the chance to exhibit the level of respect and caring that she wants students to practice.

Love of Learning and Personal Accountability

In addition to fostering an environment of respect, schools should also help students to acquire a sense of personal accountability for studying as part of the emphasis on love of learning, since learning is students' main responsibility in high school. Students learn personal accountability for their work through the demands of serious study. Thus a school fostering excellence and love of learning must be successful in creating an atmosphere in which students accept study as their normal, everyday, and most important task. A school-wide spirit of serious work is central, since excellence is achieved only by the ongoing effort to do one's best.

In the classroom, educators should identify academic goals for their students and involve the students themselves in setting those goals. Personal accountability comes with self-discipline, patience, persistence, self-evaluation, order, using time appropriately, meeting deadlines, and at least a minimal sense of duty. Holding students accountable means that faculty and administration should also work hard and be personally accountable, since they can teach accountability most effectively by their example. Teachers who expect students to hand in homework punctually have the duty to return tests and homework within a reasonable amount of time. Students will come to class on time if the teacher does, too. An administration expecting the student government to be responsible must give appropriate priority to student council requests. Coaches who require punctuality to practice must be punctual themselves. Students will usually rise to the occasion if they see that teachers and administration also value personal excellence. Lickona comments on the importance of learning to work hard by saying:

> Good schools will convey a balanced message about work by creating the kind of human environment where people clearly matter. At the same time, they will be diligent in teaching students a lesson they once knew better than they do now: To succeed in life and build a better world, they need more than brains and talent. They also need the capacity for working hard and for being personally accountable for their work. Developing that capacity must be high on the agenda of our efforts to build the character of our children. (EFC, 331)

Chapter 3
Character Education:
Single-Sex or Coeducational?

Public education in the Untied States is coeducational. The impact of this type of educational environment on school climate and on the success a character education scheme based on a love for learning and excellence cannot be ignored. Our public school administrators are becoming increasingly aware of the positive results of all-girls math and science classes, and some have taken the innovative step of offering single gender sections of these subjects so that girls feel free to strive for excellence.

The primary professional interest that prompted this research was the desire to determine the most appropriate definition and practice of character education for girls between the ages of ten and eighteen. This, of course, is not the main concern of all educators, nor is it the only way to study or to formulate character education. Educators committed to character development must work within the parameters set by their districts or schools. Keeping this in mind, the mission statements suggested in Chapter Two of this last part of the book were chosen to accommodate both single-sex and coeducational schools. The issue of co- or single-sex education is not the only factor involved in effective character education, but one must recognize that it has a major impact on school climate and upon the manner in which the character education suggested here is carried out.

Educational research provides solid evidence of the advantages of single-sex education for girls between the sixth and twelfth grades. The rest of this chapter will discuss the advantages of single-sex education for young women, based on five key characteristics of the hidden curriculum found in all schools: same-sex role modeling, the impact of a single-sex environment on girls' academic performance, opportunities for female leadership roles, teacher-student interaction, and the impact on schools of the adolescent subculture.

This study takes into account, however, that single-sex education is not an option for all girls, and the arguments presented in this section are presented as suggestions that, if and when able to be implemented, would greatly enhance the effectiveness of character education by means of the hidden curriculum. All-girls schools can readily carry out the suggestions made by Diane Rothenberg in her study *Supporting Girls in Early Adolescence* (SGEA). She wrote:

> By assuring that girls' contributions are valued in and out of the
> classroom, and by creating an environment in which girls can express

their opinions, make mistakes, and demonstrate their interest in learning without fear of harassment or of being ignored, parents, teachers, and administrators can make a positive contribution to the development of adolescent and preadolescent girls.[1]

Role Models

The first issue is that of same-sex role modeling. In American society, women, both single and married, are an accepted part of the work force. But it can be argued that determining the profile of the successful female professional is ongoing. Imitation of the successful male model has been discarded as inadequate, but the configuration of the female attributes that constitute a competent women professional have not been fully explored. According to the 1990 study of single sex high schools done by Lee and Marks,

> Women (educated in all-girls' schools) had significantly less stereotypic views of women's appropriate roles than girls from coeducational schools, especially in the workplace. As socialization has been shown elsewhere to be an important factor impeding women from nontraditional careers (e.g. in science) breaking the barriers of stereotypic attitudes among women is important.[2]

In single-sex schools, girls have the opportunity to be exposed to successful females, and especially female professionals working in a variety of positions, not solely as teachers. For example, women in single-sex schools could be expected to be in charge of the business as well as the educational aspects of the school. Girls' schools have the opportunity to further enhance modeling of successful female professionals by inviting graduates to speak about their professions and the impact an all-girls school education has had on their identity as women. In this regard, M. E. Tidball conducted an analysis of women's college graduates to determine a possible relationship between high-achieving graduates and the number of women faculty. She found a very high correlation. "This is not to say," She admits, "that an abundance of women role models is the only predictor of subsequent achievement by women students; but it does reinforce the relative importance of the relationship in comparison with other institutional variables."[3]

Diane Rothenburg also reports that

> As a group girls exhibit a general decline in science achievement not observed in boys, and this gender gap may be increasing (Backes, 1994.) The National Assessment of Educational Progress (NAEP) results indicate that for 9- and 13-year-olds, gender differences in science achievement increased between 1978 and 1986, with females' academic performance declining. It has been argued that girls in single-sex schools have the possibility of participating more successfully in class than girls in coeducational environments.[4]

In a study published in *The Career Development Quarterly*, M. I. Rubenfeld argues that in girls' schools, students were generally more interested in academics and showed significantly greater gains in reading, science, and educational ambition over the course of their high school years. These girls' schools also showed some positive effect on the students' locus of control. And these girls were less likely (than girls in coeducational schools) to see themselves in sex-stereotyped adult roles.[5]

Girls educated in a single-sex environment are expected to perform at the highest levels in all subjects: the arts and literature, as well as mathematics and sciences, subjects that are the domain of boys in coeducational settings. In his book on the pros and cons of single-sex and coeducation, *Boys and Girls in School; Together or Separate?* Cornelius Riordan comments, "Girls in single-sex schools, especially, seem to obtain higher cognitive outcomes than their counterparts in mixed-sex schools."[6]

In *Learning to Lose,* Diane Spender and Elizabeth Sarah argue:

> Although girls in single-sex schools can have a more limited selection of courses from which to choose, they will probably be much more free to choose the ones they want than they would be in a co-educational school, where they will compete with boys for the resources and also be subtly induced to satisfy traditional sex roles [T]he importance given to academic learning in a single-sex school will probably not give girls the impression that it doesn't make any difference whether or not they do well in school, a message that they may have already received through their socialization and their culture, and something which is not always contradicted in coeducational schools. Besides, girls in single-sex schools have a better chance of having women teach them mathematics and because of this, will less probably see these classes as 'masculine'.[7]

Leadership Opportunities & Teacher-Student Interaction

A single-sex school can also provide girls the opportunity to compete for and assume leadership roles that, in coeducational schools, are traditionally considered masculine. Cornelius Riordan comments again, "Coed schools not only offer fewer role models but also differentiate student roles according to sex. ... mixed schools are essentially boys' schools in as far as they are dominated by boys' interest."(GBS, 50) According to research, counselors in coeducational institutions sometimes encourage girls to choose classes based on traditional sex role activity or, because classes have limited enrollment, they encourage girls to choose courses not considered important for the future success of boys. This indirectly fosters the tendency in some girls to hold back in deference to the boys' choices. The courses usually discouraged are mathematics and the sciences.

Teacher-student interaction in the classroom is another important advantage of female single-sex education. There has been much written about teachers' unconscious inclination to favor boys in classroom interaction and to have lower expectation of girls, especially in the areas of mathematics and sciences. In her study *Separation and the Education of Women,* Joy K. Rice describes the type of classroom interaction that seems to favor boys, citing evidence that girls receive less of the teacher's time and attention in terms of number of responses, length of responses, and delay time given for student response. Boys, she asserts, command physical, psychological, and linguistic space, interrupting women's speech in mixed-sex groups and classrooms. Girls "service" boys more frequently (providing pencils, paper, food, lending money and doing homework) than boys do these same things for girls. "It does seem clear," she summarizes, "that teachers generally give more time and attention to males in classrooms."[8]

Adolescent Subculture

The adolescent subculture pervasive among high school students is the last, but not at all the least influential aspect of a school's climate that concerns us here. This subculture is an intense component of any school's culture and directly affects character education that utilizes the hidden curriculum. In his classic study entitled *The Adolescent Society,* James Coleman argues that our society has created an adolescent subculture in which popularity is sought at the expense of achievement, especially in schools. Further studies provide support for Coleman's thesis that female adolescent development is aided by single-sex schools, where greater emphasis is placed upon healthy competition in a more academic environment. Coleman points to one aspect of a school's subculture that can easily dominate all others: girls' sensitivity to boys' judgment of their appearance and their dress, and how boys fare academically in comparison to girls in class.[9]

When this kind of preoccupation dominates a school culture, fostering a climate of excellence, in which each student strives to do the best, can be almost impossible, especially if doing her best will make a girl unpopular. According to their 1991 study, M. I. Rubenfeld and F. D. Gilroy affirm that a student in a single-sex environment would have the "opportunity to compete academically without fear of alienating potential boyfriends..."[10] Diane Spender and Elizabeth Sarah also cite many instances of female dependence on male approval in the school setting.[11]

Because the adolescent subculture does not value respect and love of learning, it can have serious repercussions in a school striving for excellence. By placing high value on things unrelated to or detrimental to good character, this subculture nullifies any appreciation of learning and excellence by making the school climate seem unattractive and out of touch.[12] Therefore, to be able to educate for good character by means of the hidden curriculum, it is important to have the possibility of creating a school climate in which the adolescent subculture's influence can be lessened. In her study entitled "Education and the Individual: Schooling for Girls or Mixed Schools – A Mixed Blessing?" Jennifer Shaw writes:

> In an all-girls school, being both clever and attractive is a compatible, but not necessary combination. Such a combination may be less viable in a mixed school where, in a climate of overall anxiety about appropriate sex behavior, dichotomies are presented and choices have to be made. Little protection from, or alternatives to, failure (or success) in romantic competition are afforded.[13]

This being the case, girls may be less likely to want to strive for excellence in coeducational situations, very aware that the stigma excellence brings will jeopardize their social opportunities. Riordan cites research showing that, although it is not completely absent, all-girls schools typically have a less intense subculture of this sort than coeducational schools, and Spender and Sarah concur. They quote a graduate of an all-girls school as saying:

> Being only with women was much easier ... We got along in a different way. We didn't feel forced to compete with each other when there weren't boys around ... The feelings of solidarity that can be built when boys are not in the classroom is quite impressive. Within a single-sex framework girls can dedicate themselves to their interests without having to hide the results.[14]

The most effective environment for character education for girls seems to be one in which girls are exposed to successful female role models in all aspects of school life; a school in which girls can aspire to all types of leadership positions; an environment in which they can learn and excel academically without negative social repercussions, and in which the adolescent subculture can be subsumed to a certain extent by a challenging environment of serious work and close friendships. Thus, it would seem that a single-sex environment is a great advantage in effective character education for adolescent girls, especially one in which the hidden curriculum is used as an essential teaching tool.

Chapter 4
Creating a Tradition of Virtue

In the National Association of Secondary School Principals (NASSP) Bulletin of 1993, Charles Moore writes that "all school organizations have distinctive personalities or cultures that reflect values, beliefs, and aspirations for the students, staff members, and parents.[1] The administration and staff of schools committed to virtue education by fostering respect and love of learning must conscientiously foster a school culture that seconds the virtue education that they want to provide. In other words, there must be a purposeful and concrete planning of the hidden curriculum. The instruments available are as varied as the subjects taught, the people in the school community, and the activities promoted. Everything in a school is a possible instrument for encouraging excellence at some point in time and in some circumstance. Moore describes excellence as "the conditions that demand teachers to be excited and inquisitive about teaching, and students to be excited and inquisitive about learning…there is an excitement about teaching and learning that transcends all school activities and decisions."(66) Before considering respect and love of learning individually, however, we will discuss some aspects of the school environment that, at first glance, may not seem to be essential to a climate of excellence. Each of these aspects, however, can teach aspects of virtue not obviously part of the formal curriculum, but which are at the heart of the virtue tradition.

The School Building

Schools communicate a great deal about their expectations by the degree to which they emphasize cleanliness and neatness in public areas. Student bathrooms, hallways, the cafeteria, and lounges can add to the climate of excellence if they are kept clean and neat. In his article "Restructured Schools: How, Why Do They Work?" Charles Moore argues that cleanliness and order in a school are a sign of pride in one's profession and work. He says:

> In schools that work, all employees take pride in their work and all work is valued …from custodians who take pride in maintaining the physical plant because they know their work is valued by faculty, students and parents, to kitchen employees who prepare meals that are appreciated. (RS 64)

When a building's appearance is attractive and inviting, students and staff find it easier to aspire to excellence in their jobs of teaching and learning. Active student participation in maintaining a neat environment is also an appropriate way to foster a sense of ownership and a spirit of community.

Another way in which the school building can play an important role is the unplanned interaction with students that can occur there. Many times the serendipitous contacts when students are in the hallways can be decisive. These occasions typically arise before and after school, between classes, and during lunch. Teachers and administrators should make the effort to mingle with students in the halls because students are sensitive to casual personal encounters. Both teachers and administrators build a spirit of mutual respect and friendship through these encounters. Teachers who do not make the effort to mingle with students in informal situations give students the impression that they are uninterested in them and occupied with things rather than with people. As a result, students are less inclined to view them as role models and possible mentors. Teachers and administrators who make the effort to be in the halls and to greet students with at least a smile create a true spirit of community. It is in these informal and non-obligatory moments of friendliness that students sense the true concern of teachers and administrators.

The Principal

Researchers have found that the school principal is the most important person in an environment of respect and love of learning. All schools need persons of integrity and leadership in positions of authority, but schools striving to put the character educational ideals suggested here into practice are in special need of administrators conscious of the importance of their position. Administrators, especially the principal, need to be exemplary in the way in which they exercise authority. Faculty and students expect them to practice what they preach. Principals ought to be flexible, maintaining a spirit of teamwork with teachers as well as students. They should sustain open, two-way communication with faculty and students, and make a special effort to meet deadlines in those matters that serve as the basis of the work of others. Carl D. Glickman writes, "In order for a school to be educationally successful, it must be a community of professionals who work together toward a vision of teaching and learning that transcends individual classrooms, grades, and departments."[2]

Principals effective in fostering a tradition and climate of excellence also possess vision: an innovative, open, and forward-looking attitude toward their school and those who work and study in it. This is especially important when a school purports to foster student and teacher initiatives in school life. Without the principal's open and forward-looking attitude, both students and teachers can become stagnant, and, instead of being the upbeat and enthusiastic instrument of character education, the hidden curriculum can become restrictive and unappealing, discontent replacing an enthusiastic striving for excellence.

Hiring New Staff

Principals who encourage a climate of excellence keep character education in mind when hiring new staff. Everyone who is part of the school community creates the school's climate. Thus, teachers support a climate of excellence through their teaching, role modeling, and mentoring. In order to fit into this kind of environment, they must be enthusiastic about this particular model of character education. The effectiveness of this model of character education depends to a great extent on teachers' trying to put their best foot forward at all times, aware that they are role models more by the kind of person they are than by what they teach, even though what and how they teach is also extremely important. Roberta McKay states, "It will take character on the part of educators to have an impact on children in the area of character education." (CE, 46) Therefore, principals must look for a common understanding of and appreciation for the need of character education. Teachers who consider character education a violation of personal freedom would place the entire enterprise in jeopardy. In addition, students, aware that the school takes an official position in favor of a climate of excellence, are frequently confused when a teacher is in open disagreement with its ideals. McKay also comments "without demonstration in school of the [virtues] values we may wish children to embrace, any form of [virtue] values education program is doomed to failure." (CE, 47) The hiring process becomes more time consuming, but the stakes are very high; teachers create the climate of respect and love of learning essential for virtue education. Principals support an environment of serious work and mutual respect by expecting top quality teaching from faculty, top quality learning by students, and top quality work from themselves, maintaining a demanding, but enthusiastic tone in their own task of setting the pace in the school's character education efforts.

Teachers: Turning Theory into Reality

Although the principal is the most important person in maintaining a school-wide awareness of character education goals, understanding the role of teachers in character education is crucial. We have already seen that growth in love of learning develops primarily through serious and top quality academic work carried out in the classroom and guided by the teacher. In her research on moral values and the virtues taught and learned in the classroom, Mary Williams writes, "I expected to find that formal lessons about respect produce the best results. Yet, the findings indicate that respect is taught best through a hidden curriculum of modeling and quality teaching that creates a positive moral climate."[3]

Teachers are not an appendage to character education in schools that aim to create a climate of love of learning; they are its primary agents. Their professional competence and academic expectations are the norm by which students judge the value of their own work and the seriousness with which to view character education itself. Williams further found that "character education manifests itself in teacher practice as respect for each student as a responsible, active learner. Model teachers understand that students require an environment of mutual trust and respect."[4]

Virtue in the Classroom

As we saw in the section devoted to Alasdair MacIntyre, practices have specific purposes and concrete standards that must be met to accomplish their purposes. Practices demand a specific level of perfection from participants if they want to be successful. When they accept the challenge, participants make the effort to acquire the virtues they need, even if they may not think of their activity in terms of virtue acquisition. Thus, when teachers stipulate standards of excellence in their classes, they also require virtuous student behavior in order to be successful.

Because of the vital role they play in virtue education, it is important that teachers think of their classes in two ways: as integral parts of the larger context of the school (Macintyre's notion of traditions) and as the occasion for fostering respect and love of learning (Macintyre's notion of practices). Although students may attend a school whose school-wide hidden curriculum encourages them to value respect and love of learning, they actually learn to live virtue within the classroom.

To understand this idea in a practical way, teachers should think of their classes as practices embedded within the context of the school and its traditions. Their classes both participate in and contribute to the school's character education tradition. Each teacher strengthens the message of respect and love of learning because students absorb it inside her classroom as well as in the school as a whole.

When teachers realize how much the school relies on them to convey the character message to the students, they use respect and love of learning as their reference point for carrying out diverse activities and teaching. Teachers understand that they, more than the administration, maintain and enrich the school's character tradition when they make the effort to cultivate a caring environment in their classes that involves accountability, respect, and love of learning. Virtue education fostered by means of the hidden curriculum relies heavily upon teachers' common commitment to the school's character tradition.

Co-curricular Activities

In *The Rehabilitation of Virtue,* Robert Sandin writes, "We must also allow virtue to arise serendipitously from the manifold experience of learning. There is no area ... where occasion is not presented for considering the highest ideals for human life and character ... in the non-curricular experience of schooling, too." (RV, 208)

According to Edwin and Kevin Ryan in *Reclaiming our Schools,* when a school's hidden curriculum fosters excellence, cocurricular activities are a very important character tool. These activities are an effective way to help students become contributing members of the school community, an essential characteristic of respect.

> Studies have found that involvement in extracurricular activities is a
> better predictor of later-life success than good grades ... Many adult
> roles require people to work closely with and get along with others.
> Compromise and display both initiative and obedience – the sorts of
> behaviors involved in prosocial conduct ... Students practicing pro-
> social conduct are partly being trained for such later roles in everyday
> work. (ROS 62)

Involvement in cocurricular activities is also one way in which teachers can exercise their role as mentors, since these activities, more than the classroom, are an excellent opportunity to initiate personal relationships with students. Wynne and Ryan note the attraction teachers feel for this type of contact.

> [These activities are a] challenging and rewarding responsibility for
> many educators. It often requires a subtle mix of inspiration, direc-
> tion, and even moral counseling. Some educators became teachers
> precisely because they wanted to carry out such responsibilities. Or-
> ganizing such activities requires imagination, commitment, planning,
> and insight." (ROS 62)

Among the variety of cocurricular activities possible, service-learning deserves special mention, because of its important role in teaching respect for other members of the community. A school offering a variety of service opportunities aimed at differing interests and talents such as peer tutoring, school office helpers, visits to the house-bound elderly, teaches that all of these ways of being of service are important, and that they, students, should be of service to others. Service is an experience that interests and challenges them, encourages critical thinking, and stimulates them to contribute in areas of passionate interest.

As all educators realize, athletics can also have a powerful influence on a young person's sense of respect. The gym teacher or coach can be a natural mentor for young athletes. It is not surprising that the coach's office is frequently the place athletes go when they have free time. A coach committed to fostering excellence can be of great help in making excellence appealing to students. Wynne and Ryan did an informal survey of high school students and found the following results:

> A sample of pupils from several different high schools were asked
> which type of faculty member they would consult if they had a seri-
> ous problem. Both boys and girls overwhelmingly preferred a gym
> teacher or sports coach ... we assume that the students were express-
> ing support for a 'coachlike' style of interaction ... good coaches
> have to know how to emotionally reach and motivate players, to
> stimulate them to go the last mile, and beyond. That is no small tal-
> ent. (ROS, 122)

Continuity of Expectations

The central role that teachers play in character education is further highlighted by the way in which students learn virtue. MacIntyre says that practices specify which virtues are learned - each practice has concrete standards for successful completion of the tasks involved. If participants in the practice want to be successful, they will make the effort to acquire the virtues that permit success. Thus, when teachers determine standards for academic excellence, they are actually deciding what virtues students will need to do well academically.

Although each subject area has its own particular requirements, teachers realize that they have common expectations in many areas. All teachers undoubtedly expect students to be self-disciplined, to complete homework on time, to share, to follow class rules, to be cooperative during class discussions, to be honest, etc. All of these virtues are important to loving to learn and being respectful.

When we say that practices lean on each other, we mean that teachers can count on each other to uphold the virtue tradition by agreeing to expect all students to display the same virtues. This common understanding binds teachers together. It also helps students to learn virtue. Since virtues are developed over time and through repetition, the more teachers who expect the same good habits, the better chance the students have of really growing in virtue.

Teachers and the Mission Statement

In addition to having each one's inner sense of their importance in the personal development of their students, teachers understand the role that virtue education plays in their school because the philosophy and mission statements spell it out for them. As a result, the school mission and philosophy statements are even more important than the character education tradition.

I was walking in the hall one day, close to the classroom where a second-year teacher was engaging her class in an ethics lesson. As I approached her door I heard her say, "Have you noticed the posters in the halls? Well, this story is going to show us one way to show respect. That is our school theme this year." This teacher had identified personally with the theme of respect and she used it to introduce a new piece of literature. Her character lesson was not based on ready-made materials about respect. Its effectiveness lay in the seemingly spontaneous insertion of the school's tradition into her classroom interaction with students in such a natural way that it seemed to be a matter of chance. But, of course, it was not. That teacher considers herself a teacher of character and she enters every class with that attitude. She considers herself an important part of the school-wide tradition of respect and love of learning.

When teachers engage their students as this young teacher did, they understand their role in character education. As we have said before, teachers are at the heart of creating and enriching a school's tradition. When teachers see their classrooms as practices that participate in the school's tradition of excellence, their efforts to create a climate of respect and love of learning become the basis of the broader climate that permeates the entire school.

A strong school-wide tradition has a great influence on teacher expectations. Teachers who view themselves as teachers of character as well as purveyors of information include character growth in their definition of a "good student." An upper-level math teacher in my building once said that, even though one of her students had excellent math skills, she did not consider her to be her best student because she had not demonstrated a commitment to virtue. As she saw it, a student exhibiting only strong math ability had not learned everything necessary to be a good math student. For teachers who foster character, being virtuous is an integral part of being a good student, and being as good a student as one can be is an integral part of being a virtuous person.

The Privilege of Being a Teacher

Teachers are in a privileged position with regard to virtue education. Formal schooling lends itself to fostering some virtues that students may not have the opportunity to learn in other circumstances. For example, outside of school students may not have the opportunity to learn expertise, a virtue Lickona considers key to growing in love of learning. In *Educating for Character* he comments:

> If students never have the experience of taking hold of a subject and probing it deeply ... they never know the structure of a field of knowledge or the rewards of in-depth learning. And they don't develop the intellectual discipline needed to produce new knowledge... Developing expertise through in-depth learning is one more way to translate high teacher expectations into children's educational experience. (EFC, 217)

Children may not have to meet deadlines on a regular basis outside of school. Teachers frequently comment that the first lesson that many students learn is to complete and to turn in daily homework. The second lesson is budgeting their time well on long-term projects. This kind of planning, required by long-term projects, may be an experience that students have only in school. Doing quality work on a regular basis may also be another virtue that students will develop only at school. When they expect good quality homework consistently and teach students to take the time necessary to produce it, teachers also help students learn self-discipline and orderly work habits. Lickona has this to say:

> Good schools will convey a balanced message about work by creating the kind of human environment where people clearly matter. At the same time they will be diligent in teaching students a lesson they once knew better than they do now: To succeed in life and build a better world, they need more than brains and talent, they also need the capacity for working hard. Developing that capacity must be high on the agenda of our efforts to build the character of our children. (EFC, 227)

Yet another virtue that students may learn primarily in school is the virtue of respect. There are some aspects of respect that young people experience principally in school - such as working comfortably in a large group of peers and learning that hard work is part of meaningful participation in a group. A child's school experience is very important in developing virtue and teachers should be encouraged to recognize their privileged role, especially when other adults do not have the same opportunity.

Teachers as Role Models

Restricting the teacher's role in virtue education to expecting students to meet standards of excellence in work would be a fundamental mistake, however. Teachers who are role models of excellence should expect excellence from their students, but more importantly, they should also demand excellence from themselves. As part of her research, Mary Williams asked students to describe quality teachers. Students replied:

> They present clear, consistent, and sincere messages; do not pull rank - are never authoritarian; they communicate high expectations; really listen; communicate their commitment through actions; are hardworking and really care about student learning [5]

Effective character education teachers come to class well-prepared and ready to be an example of the enthusiasm they want to elicit from their students. Students' enthusiasm and engagement in learning parallel the enthusiasm and commitment shown by teachers. Thus, teachers of excellence give special importance to being fair in their dealings with students as a group, while at the same time being kind and understanding with students individually. Teachers of excellence create a community spirit among the students and between themselves and the class as a whole. In writing of schools that have successfully reformed their school climate, Charles Moore asserts, "In these schools there's a feeling of respect, safety, and support of learning. Students are cared for, and as a result there is an increased potential to learn more effectively. Students relate to adults in healthy and positive ways." (RS, 67)

To turn the theory of character education into reality, teachers must see themselves as educating for good character even more than teaching concrete academic material. When modeling personal excellence and setting standards of excellence for their students, teachers not only participate in the climate of excellence fostered in the school-wide hidden curriculum, they actually create that climate and support it by their personal commitment.

This reality makes education a most challenging profession, for success in teaching excellence is not the result merely of professional competence. Success as a teacher depends heavily on personal integrity and effort, a combination not always required by other professions.

Chapter 5

School and Family: Creating a Community of Shared Interests

School and Society

Before addressing issues of the family/school community, we must look at the relationship of schools to society. This is the last of the major themes that Dewey and MacIntyre write about in relation to education. Both view education as a tool to further social identification. Dewey's concept of education is aimed at reconstructing democracy. MacIntyre sees education as a tool for cultural continuity, and because he does not consider liberalism a legitimate cultural framework, he argues that the only alternative is to turn to small communities in which one can go about life undisturbed by the larger liberal society.

American society is pluralistic, and it is within this context that we, who live at the beginning of the twenty-first century, must play out our lives. The American social structure will not change within the lifetime of parents who need to educate their children now or that of professionals who are now educators. Thus, we must determine how to educate young people today so that they can lead fruitful and happy lives within these circumstances. Although the question of what is best for American society has been at the heart of this research, this study has not discussed the best way to guarantee the continuity of liberalism and pluralism; nor has it tried to find a secluded niche for an alternative mentality. The main concern has been individual lives, those who find themselves in American society as it is and whose concern is living well within it. Thus, the last section of this book has attempted to formulate a character education model that offers a realistic way of cultivating high ideals in young people living in mainstream America.

The children and adults who strive to be virtuous are the citizens that America's liberal and pluralistic society needs. They are able to build bridges among diverse groups because they are firmly rooted in their own identity. They are able to recognize values that they hold in common with differing value systems without losing their own perspective precisely because they know that the good comes in many forms and from many places.

Virtue education helps students write the narrative story of their lives by providing the kind of guidance that helps them discern what is good for them and the virtues that they need to pursue that good. This is Alasdair MacIntyre's argument and it is as valid for those wanting to be part of American pluralism as it is for those who prefer living on its outskirts.

Students do not generally aspire to live in isolated communities such as those envisioned by MacIntyre. Most of them want to form part of the larger American society.[1] That society is a pluralistic one and unless character education helps them live within it, it will have failed. As F. Clark Power puts it in *The Challenge of Pluralism*, the narrative of their lives ought to be a responsible "engagement of pluralism." He gives a clear idea of the task of character education when he defines pluralism as "both unity and diversity, the one nation existing in multiple forms or parts...a pluralism of value systems distinguishable from mere diversity in customs, language, food, etc."[2]

Character Education in a Pluralistic Society

Character education ought to prepare students to live alongside those who come from distinct traditions and value systems, for a healthy pluralism shelters within it differing world views, each one a strong local community with well-established traditions and values. William Damon also feels that engagement of the prevalent social atmosphere is crucial to the construction of a life that makes sense in the modern world:

> Communities cannot be preserved through attempts to seal themselves off from outsiders. This is a losing effort. Eventually the wall will break down. Those who are unprepared for interacting constructively with the full range of people in our diverse society will be unable to adapt. (GE, 233)

Pluralism can exist only if each value system or tradition has deep roots in its own way of life. It is this multiplicity of communities or traditions that strengthens pluralism. David Popenoe stresses the importance of attachment to traditions and practices in establishing a sense of personal worth and value, especially in a pluralistic society. He writes,

> Our social problems are not due nearly as much to the competition of loyalties as to their absence...they are due to alienation, loss of belonging, not having affiliations about which one deeply cares. A major task of our age, therefore, is this: while seeking to maximize individual development...we must at the same time maintain some semblance of tribalism – which boils down to protecting and cultivating the primordial institutions of family and community.[3]

Citizens of a pluralistic society, then, should seek out an education for their children that encourages them to love and to better the traditions into which they have been born. At the same time, they must maintain an open attitude toward those goods they have in common with other traditions. In his article, "Pluralism, Virtues, and the Post-Kohlbergian Era in Moral Psychology," Daniel K. Lapsley writes that pluralism needs citizens who can "navigate their way through the morass of pluralistic conceptions of good lives such that a life of personal integrity...can be maintained."[4] This is no small task. Young people need an education that not only offers information but that also helps them to love and to live within their traditions and their own value systems. It is of greatest importance that students be educated in this way. As Powers pointed out, however, integrating the young into their local communities and traditions should never be reduced to cooking local foods, speaking the language of their parents or dressing in a specific way. Traditions, understood as MacIntyre conceived them, can house a great diversity of customs, languages, and foods while remaining strong and vibrant. David Popenoe sums up the need of these traditions by saying:

> Put another way, our natural inclination is to want to have close personal ties and to be included in strong groups that have clear values and a stable social structure; a social situation which can provide us with a sense of identity and belonging. The strength of social ties varies from culture to culture around the world. Studies of these cultures have shown that the stronger the social ties, the fewer the social and personal problems. (RD, 84)

Virtue education may not be widely understood or practiced at this moment, but this should not be cause for concern. Configured as it is today, American society can only be enriched as the virtue tradition grows stronger. What is essential, however, is that virtue education be available to parents who want their children to grow in virtue on their way to living good and happy lives.

The Family/School Interest Community

According to David Popenoe, American pluralism is no longer so much a matter of geographic division, as it is of valuation division, and members of the same value system frequently do not live in the same geographic location. In discussing this phenomenon, Popenoe outlines ways of fostering community based on common values:

> There are two broad approaches to fostering community in America. One focuses on residential areas... The other focuses on nonresidential 'interest' communities, or groups of people who live apart from one another but who constitute a network of social interaction and who share common interests and values. This second approach is the one gradually being played out in America. (RD, 84, 88-9)

Using Popenoe's second definition of community, public and private schools committed to virtue education can often be considered nonresidential interest communities, part of the *one nation existing in multiple parts* of which Power spoke above. This realization should spur such schools to seek out parents who can become members of their interest community. These schools would do well to make themselves known, seeking out like-minded parents and teachers. They will grow in strength and stability as they discover additional community members.

In addition to the virtue education community's efforts to discover its members, potential community participants need to "discover themselves," so to speak. Take, for example, parents who are unaware of virtue education, but who would appreciate it if they knew of the option. These potential members of the "virtue community" were students of Values Clarification and moral reasoning, neither of which provided much guidance in learning to grow in virtue.

Unless their families or their faith traditions educate them differently, these parents are often unsure of the orientation and the meaning of their own lives. Wolfgang Brezinska writes, "What characterizes our society as a whole, the social isolation, the individualization of ideals and life style …is naturally to be found among parents.[5]

Schools must be at the heart of this effort to introduce parents to virtue education. To do so, they must be cognizant of their responsibility to establish themselves as interest communities, not simply as alternative options. Not doing so could deprive those unaware of virtue education of participating in a tradition from which they and their children could benefit. To advance the virtue education tradition requires specific planning. There are many ways to introduce potential community members. One way would be to offer seminars and to study the philosophical foundations of virtue education. Another, unscientifically termed the "empirical" method, would probably attract more parents, however.

For parents of the twenty-first century, the "empirical" method may be the best and simplest way for them to discover virtue education. This applies to public schools as well as private schools. Although some private schools may have their character education more explicitly formulated, public schools have character goals as well.

To evaluate the effectiveness of the options that exist for them, parents should take a serious look at all of the elements that make up character education, especially virtue education – the students, teachers, staff and environment. They should make the effort to meet students. What attitude do they have toward their school? With how much enthusiasm do they talk about their school and of what do they complain? Students are adolescents, of course, and so some complaining is to be expected, but students who have understood virtue should be able to distinguish between objective and subjective limitations and defects. By talking with students and teachers, parents can decide whether to become part of a school's character tradition.

Parents will know whether or not they want their children to be like the students they see and whether or not they would like those teachers to educate their children. In most cities, the public school system has a variety of options for parents, albeit limited: charter schools, academies of differing orientations, etc. All parents, no matter where their children go to school should try to know the environment, students, faculty, and staff that will influence their children's character growth.

When parents choose virtue education, they join the community of families, administrators, and faculty who have chosen virtue education as their common interest. This mutual commitment is essential for the growth of children and adolescents, and it is an integral part of the strength of the family/school community. As Damon asserts, "Institutions like school and family establish a community for raising children only when they collaborate effectively with one another." (GE, 224) Although the family/school interest community has been defined as nonresidential, there is no reason to exclude the possibility of its existence among many residents of a given neighborhood or within the community surrounding the school. Virtue education is especially appealing to young parents who live in all kinds of neighborhoods and who have all types of children. It provides an environment in which students of all abilities will learn to strive to do their best and acquire an active spirit of social involvement.

Parents not exposed to virtue education in their own schooling frequently want it for their children. In his interview with Yepes Stork, MacIntyre suggested as much. He argued that people who know nothing of philosophy frequently act in an Aristotelian manner to keep a job, to reduce tensions in a marriage, or to bring children up well. Virtue is a natural response to life's exigencies. It may well be that the majority of parents today fall within this category. (DV, 89) Thus, the considerations of this chapter lead back to the initial discussion in the first chapter of Part I. The introductory discussion began by examining character education's philosophical foundations and describing students who had been educated well in the Kantian, Kohlbergian, and Aristotelian traditions. Although studying the philosophical foundations of character education does not seem to be the best procedure at this time, schools that present their students to prospective parents as a way of demonstrating how virtue education can help them are in fact, providing parents with a hands-on philosophical lesson, the same one suggested at the beginning of this book. When looking for the best way to live, there seems no way to avoid philosophy in some way, shape or form.

The School's Contribution to the Family/School Interest Community

When the family/school community has been established, the school in its role as an expert educational organization must collaborate with parents in creating the tradition of virtue education in their homes, thereby strengthening the bonds between family and school. The school's collaborative efforts can be divided into three areas: offering parents professional expertise in character education, establishing school-family communication, and fostering teamwork between school and family.

The school as an expert institution and teachers as expert professionals have experience in character education far broader than that of parents. This experience, coupled with the philosophy and mission statements, puts the school and its faculty in the center of cultivating and sustaining the values of the family/school community. The wealth of knowledge accrued over the years by the school should be placed at the service of parents so that they can foster virtue at home. The school should provide parents the opportunity to attend parenting workshops and seminars, in which some of the following topics could be discussed: age-appropriate consideration of virtue acquisition, practical suggestions on the use of computers, CDs, radio, and television, suggestions to help teach and reinforce good study habits in the home, reading materials for parents, age-appropriate reading lists for students, fostering generous participation in family life, etc.

Personal Communication

Personal communication is essential if the community is to remain strong and united. In addition to meeting with parents as community, the school must remember that it has the responsibility of promoting a commitment to community traditions in school and at home by fostering personal communication between the professionals in school and parents individually.

One useful way to connect with parents personally is the parent-teacher conference. In these conferences, teachers can suggest ways to use specific virtues so that students will be successful in their academic efforts.

Another important tool for reaching parents one by one is the parent-mentor or parent-advisor conference. Parents and mentors use this time to talk over ways in which they can address the child's overall struggles rather than focusing on academics only.

Teamwork

The last important element in creating and maintaining a strong community of interest is teamwork. It is very true that the school and its professionals have little contact with students in comparison with the time they spend with their families. If one considers character education in terms of amount of time dedicated to the children, Dewey was correct in saying that the school is at the bottom of the list in character education. Schools do not necessarily have continued contact with students beyond the years of formal schooling, nor do they have the same responsibility as parents do for students' overall welfare. An organization cannot replace the family. Edwin Delattre comments,

> How are we to restore the intellectual depth, the humility, and the understanding of character formation essential to a common commitment to fostering good character in the young? The first and most important answer lies with the family, whether traditional, single-parent, nuclear, or extended. Parents are a child's first and often most influential teachers. A sound home environment and loving adults have always been the strongest influence.[6]

But schools can be placed at the top of the list in another sense. A school specializing in character education should be more knowledgeable in this area than other character-forming environments, and therefore schools have the responsibility of providing information to parents and helping families carry out the character development of their children. In their article "Building Successful Home/School Partnerships," David Rosenthal and Julanne Young Sawyers comment, "Teamwork and collaboration are more likely to achieve positive results than when school systems and families work alone."[7] Schools committed to character education have the responsibility of forging communities that offer families support and expertise that help them raise children to be good, smart, and happy. Delattre comments, "Schools that sustain the best efforts of parents have likewise been a source of strength and opportunity for children to achieve both good character and good judgment."[8]

School, Religion and Character Education

Early American character education took place within the framework of religious education. In the nineteenth century, however, with the advent of the common school, Protestant denominations differing on doctrinal issues had to come to a consensus regarding the part that doctrinal education would play in public education. The result was an agreement to teach basic Christian morality in common schools, leaving doctrinal issues for Sundays. Each church taught its own tenets to its own congregation. From that time forward, schools separated character from religious education and placed character development under local governments, the agencies responsible for supervising public education. One consequence of that decision was the establishment of alternative systems of education in the middle of the 1800s. Begun first by the Catholic Church, other religious groups soon followed suit. They wanted to teach character within the framework of their religious creeds.

In contemporary America, there are many children educated in faith-based schools. These schools support the Catholic Church's original conviction that character is best taught within the context of religious belief. This conviction has important educational consequences, and therefore deserves further comment.

Character Education in Faith-based Schools

Today's faith-based schools do not think of character education as the exclusive goal of instruction, as was most often the case in Colonial America. Religious schools argue that character formation is a fundamental part of religious practice - so important that they provide an educational environment in which children learn good character within the framework of their religious beliefs.[9]

As a result, these schools have several characteristics that deserve further examination. The first is the emphasis on theological teachings. Theology outlines an understanding of the person and the purpose and goal of life for administration, teachers, and parents. They prepare the ground for understanding the need for and the purposes of education and serve as a solid foundation upon which to build effective character education.

The second characteristic worth noting is that religious creeds not only teach what a person is, but they also give a clear idea of the characteristics of a good person and the goal of a good person's life. In his book *Raising Good Children*, Lickona comments, "Traditional religion tells us who we are, why we're here, and where we're going."[10] This teleological view of life is the reason that faith-based schools consider character education essential to the educational process. These schools teach not only their own doctrinal tenets but also the qualities a good person will possess because of those beliefs. In these schools, virtue is universally considered an essential part of putting religious beliefs into practice. One can argue, therefore, that belief systems give added weight to the philosophical argument that virtue is essential to leading a good and happy life.

The third feature that strengthens the impact of character education in faith-based schools is the added motivation that religious conviction offers students in their efforts to be virtuous. Faith-based schools and the educators who teach in them encourage students to lead virtuous lives not only because they will be happy, but also because virtuous behavior is advocated by God. Wanting to please the God that they worship and love can make all the difference when children and teens pass through innumerable critical moments in which theological or philosophical logic may not convince. William Damon, who writes extensively about children's innate spirituality and religiosity, says that religious faith assures children that "there must be a larger meaning [spurring them on to] a resolute persistence even when intellectual tools such as logic have been exhausted." (GE, 89)

Although faith-based schools have a deep sense of solidarity and community spirit fostered by their common beliefs, these schools frequently have students of different religious backgrounds or no religious background at all. Families who are not part of the faith community but who, in spite of this, send their children to these schools, do so because religious schools frequently provide better academic and character education. Lickona comments on this phenomenon: "Many parents who aren't sure of their own religious beliefs nevertheless take their children to church or synagogue and send them to religious classes or schools," he asserts. "They reason: 'I'm not sure what I believe, but I want my child to have a chance to make up his own mind, and I want him to have the benefit of a good moral framework while he's growing up."[11]

These families do not participate in the out-of-school community, nor do these students have the advantage of religiously backed character education. Therefore, faith-based schools would be wise to avoid teaching good character exclusively by means of religious instruction. This would not only deprive students who are not members of the faith community of growing in character by intentional guidance, but it would signal a fundamental misconception of the nature of virtue education itself.

The True Foundation of Virtue Education

Although religious instruction does include instruction in virtue, it is important to bear in mind that virtue is not desirable because of religious belief alone. Aristotle, a Greek philosopher and pagan, was the first to write of the theory of virtue and its importance. Living a virtuous life is important for all human beings, and religious creeds substantiate this fact by their insistence on its central role in the life of faith. If schools teach virtue solely as a part of religious instruction and base it only on theological arguments, students who do not form part of the faith community could easily conclude that virtuous life is necessary only for those of a specific religion or generally for those people who believe in God.

These schools should try to clarify the true basis of the need of virtue – human nature – by considering a character education strategy that combines the teachings of their religious creeds and the strategies suggested here. This combination would place faith-based schools in a very powerful position to teach character. Theirs would be schools of respect and love of learning for all students. Students would learn to strive for excellence in every class and, in addition, learn to be good members of their religious community.

CONCLUSION

The need for character education is just as real today as it was in early America and at the time of John Dewey. Like Dewey, contemporary educators have the task of designing a character education that will prepare young people for the future. Borrowing some insights from John Dewey and some definitions from Alasdair MacIntyre, the present study has joined those who advocate virtue education in schools by means of the hidden curriculum.

This is a view of character education that will help students today and ready them for participation in a society that expects them to be autonomous but at the same time, to be committed to bettering the society that they have inherited.

Part I gave an overview of the origin of the perceived need of character education and the methods that early settlers used when trying to educate their children in virtue.

It may surprise some to know that the separation of character formation from education and religion was unheard of until the middle of the nineteenth century. In our early history reading the Bible and learning to write were the tools used to build good character: good character and religion went hand-in-hand. Religion and public schools went hand-in-hand, too, until the immigration of people who were not Protestant. Run by mainstream Protestant denominations, public school had to reduce the amount of religious instruction in the 1830s for the sake of peaceful co-existence with these new immigrants. The understanding that good character and, consequently, character education were necessary originated in a religious orientation toward life rather than in the needs of society.

By the end of the nineteenth century the impact of liberalism and urbanization on American society broke the interdependence of good character and religion. The rapid pace and constant change characteristic of industrialized life made new demands for which previous experience had not prepared the American people. The stability afforded by religious conviction and proper behavior now seemed out of place. Workers were increasingly involved in activities in which religion seemed to play no part and in which old-time proper behavior was not always encouraged. American society was assuming a new liberal identity dependent on skills and on autonomy.

The industrialization and liberalism that swept across America affected our educational system as well. John Dewey's educational philosophy was fundamental in molding American education to fit the liberal ideal. A convinced liberal himself, Dewey held that American education needed to be reconstructed to keep abreast of the new strains placed on city dwellers and rural citizens alike: the life styles of both were deeply affected by modernization. He did all that he could to restructure education, schools, and especially character training, adapting them to his conception of the urgent needs of American liberal democracy.

Dewey's concept of education as growth and his ideas regarding the purpose of education transformed basic assumptions about the purpose of education and the nature of morality in twentieth century America.

Although Dewey is currently being studied in the academy with renewed interest, having gone in and out of fashion many times since he originally set down his ideas, his influence at the practical level has fluctuated much less. Educating children to be good citizens in a democratic society has been and continues to be the backbone of American elementary and secondary education. Dewey's seminal idea, education as growth, gave rise to the idea that character education is educating young democratic citizens to assume the task of bettering society. Thus, since the beginning of the twentieth century, character education was mainly concerned with solving social problems that threatened the stability of the American democracy.

Since the 1960s, researchers have turned more often to psychology rather than to philosophy in search of principles for character education models. The most recent strategies, centering on self-knowledge and self-understanding, are evidence of this. Contemporary character education is still marked by a restless search for a worldview within the liberal tradition that will effectively help American youth overcome the serious moral problems that seem to be on the rise.

Because the liberal tradition of character education continues to search for an effective orientation, this study has stepped outside its framework into another view of good character, that of Alasdair MacIntyre. MacIntyre is not an educational philosopher *per se*, but his ideas suggest a worldview that offers a striking alternative, transcending both the exigencies and the limitations of liberal thought.

MacIntyre's philosophy defines person, education, good character, and society as the subject, the means, and the environment of a life-long narrative quest for the good. The task of education is to equip students with the dispositions of soul (virtue) that will help them initiate and continue this journey. For MacIntyre, education is education in virtue and his theory of practices and traditions give virtue a home in which to grow.

Part IV proposed a character education model that has tapped into one of Dewey's ideas; character is formed twenty-four hours a day. As for defining the essential elements of education, this model uses MacIntyre's definitions of person, human nature, education, virtue, and society. These definitions provide a more profound and realistic reflection of daily life. As a result, this chapter advocates character education by means of the hidden curriculum (Dewey) by creating a climate in which students are encouraged to become virtuous persons (MacIntyre).

The importance of social milieu in character formation supported this model's claim that a school-wide emphasis on excellence through a tradition of respect and love for learning can be very effective in making excellence attractive to adolescent students. Special mention was made of the physical environment, the principal, interaction between students and teachers, and cocurricular activities.

The model of character education advocated here helps teachers to deepen their participation in the character education process because they view their classrooms as the practices advocated by MacIntyre and their schools as the traditions within which their classes find orientation and added meaning. This model depends on teachers and the school community to help each student strive for personal, social, and intellectual excellence.

Part IV also discussed school philosophy and mission statements, two documents that help establish a stable, school-wide consensus about the nature of character education. Schools also have a responsibility to foster cultural continuity, and thus virtue education must think about its place within a liberal and pluralistic society. The ensuing discussion of the nature of community and of pluralism highlighted the value of virtue education in a pluralistic society.

Character education in schools is not effective, however, unless supported by parents as well, and so the contributions that schools can make to parent initiatives in this area were also examined.

Faith-based schools cannot be ignored, especially in a discussion of goodness and excellence. These schools are in a unique position, for much of the philosophical foundations that public education must search for are inherent in religious creeds.

Classroom techniques are neither the foundation nor the strength of this model of character education. Virtue education is not a compromise with practicality in which theory takes second place to new and improved methodologies. Concrete classroom methodologies were not mentioned at all because teachers who understand the principles of virtue education are more than capable of determining the most effective ways of turning virtue theory into classroom reality.

Unfortunately, many teachers have had minimal exposure to educational theory. Hopefully philosophical thinking has come closer to them through this study so that they can combine practical experience with theoretical considerations. When teachers have the chance to combine theory and practice they cease being simply the tools of new methodologies and truly become educators of character.

Abbreviations

This is a list of abbreviations used within the text when there are several citations within one chapter from the same work. If the work is cited frequently throughout the book, its abbreviation is used in every chapter in which the work is referenced.

AP	*The American Philosopher*
AV	*After Virtue*
CE	"Character Education: a Question of Character"
CT	"Character Training for Youth"
DD	*Dumbing Down our Kids*
DE	*Democracy and Education*
DV	"Después de la virtud"
EC	*Educar ciudadanos*
EE	*Experience and Education*
EFC	*Educating for Character*
EHW	*Educational History of the Western World*
ELW	*Ethics in Late Works*
EMW	*Ethics in Middle Works*
GBS	*Girls and Boys in School: Together or Separate?*
GE	*Greater Expectations*
HSV	*How to Seem Virtuous Without Really Being So*
IDV	*In a Different Voice*
LM	*The Life and Mind of John Dewey*
LR	"Letter to Readers" in *In a Different Voice*
LSK	*Lectures on School-Keeping*
ME	*American Education: The Metropolitan Experience*
MP	*Moral Principles in Education*
NE	*American Education: The National Experience*
NE1	*Nicomachean Ethics, Book 1*
PMD	*Philosophy of Moral Development*
PO	*Principles, Origin and Establishment of the Catholic School System*
PR	"A Partial Response to my Critics"
RD	"Roots of Declining Social Virtue"
ROS	*Reclaiming Our Schools*
RP	*Reconstruction of Philosophy*
RS	*"Reconstructed Schools: How, Why do They Work?"*
RV	*The Rehabilitation of Virtue, Foundations of Moral Education*
SS	*The School and Society*
SSC	*Schools and the Shaping of Character*
TCE	*American Education: The Colonial Experience*
TV	"Tradición y virtud"

I have divided the writings referenced into two sections. The first section contains all of the works of John Dewey that I have cited in the text of this book. It is not meant to be an exhaustive compilation of all of Dewey's writings. The second section includes the works of Alasdair MacIntyre referred to in the text plus the general bibliography.

I. WORKS OF JOHN DEWEY

Boydston, J. A., ed. *The Complete Works of John Dewey 1882-1953.* 37 vols. Carbondale: Southern Illinois University Press, 1969-1990.

Dewey, John. "The Place of Religious Emotion." Early Works Vol. 1 of *The Complete Works of John Dewey 1882-1953.* Carbondale: Southern Illinois University Press, 1969-1990.

_____. "Self-Realization as the Moral Ideal." Early Works Vol. 4 of *The Complete Works of John Dewey 1882-1953.* Carbondale: Southern Illinois University Press, 1969-1990.

_____. "My Pedagogic Creed." Early Works Vol. 5 of *The Complete Works of John Dewey 1882-1953.* Carbondale: Southern Illinois University Press, 1969-1990.

_____. *The School and Society.* Middle Works Vol. 1 of *The Complete Works of John Dewey 1882-1953.* Carbondale: Southern Illinois University Press, 1969-1990.

_____. *Studies in Logical Theory.* Middle Works Vol. 2 of *The Complete Works of John Dewey 1882-1953.* Carbondale: Southern Illinois University Press, 1969-1990.

_____. *Moral Principles in Education.* Middle Works Vol. 14 of *The Complete Works of John Dewey 1882-1953.* Carbondale: Southern Illinois University Press, 1969-1990.

_____. *Ethics (1908).* Middle Works Vol. 5 of *The Complete Works of John Dewey 1882-1953.* Carbondale: Southern Illinois University Press, 1969-1990.

_____. *Democracy and Education.* Middle Works Vol. 9 of *The Complete Works of John Dewey 1882-1953.* Carbondale: Southern Illinois University Press, 1969-1990.

_____. "Theories of Morals." Middle Works Vol. 9 of *The Complete Works of John Dewey 1882-1953.* Carbondale: Southern Illinois University Press, 1969-1990.

_____. "The Need of an Industrial Education in an Industrial Society." Middle Works Vol. 10 of *The Complete Works of John Dewey 1882-1953.* Carbondale: Southern Illinois University Press, 1969-1990.

_____. "Education and Social Direction." Middle Works Vol. 11 of *The Complete Works of John Dewey 1882-1953*. Carbondale: Southern Illinois University Press, 1969-1990.

_____. *Reconstruction of Philosophy*. Middle Works Vol. 12 of *The Complete Works of John Dewey 1882-1953*. Carbondale: Southern Illinois University Press, 1969-1990.

_____. *Human Nature and Conduct*. Middle Works Vol. 14 of of *The Complete Works of John Dewey 1882-1953*. Carbondale: Southern Illinois University Press, 1969-1990.

_____. "Social Purposes of Education." Middle Works Vol. 15 of of *The Complete Works of John Dewey 1882-1953*. Carbondale: Southern Illinois University Press, 1969-1990.

_____. *Experience and Nature*. Late Works Vol. 1 of *The Complete Works of John Dewey 1882-1953*. Carbondale: Southern Illinois University Press, 1969-1990.

_____. *The Quest for Certainty: A Study of the Relation of Knowledge and Action*. Late Works Vol. 4 of *The Complete Works of John Dewey 1882-1953*. Carbondale: Southern Illinois University Press, 1969-1990.

_____. *Individualism, Old and New*. Late Works Vol. 5 of *The Complete Works of John Dewey 1882-1953*. Carbondale: Southern Illinois University Press, 1969-1990.

_____. "What I Believe." Late Works Vol. 5 of *The Complete Works of John Dewey 1882-1953*. Carbondale: Southern Illinois University Press, 1969-1990.

_____. *Ethics (1932)*. Late Works Vol. 7 of *The Complete Works of John Dewey 1882-1953*. Carbondale: Southern Illinois University Press, 1969-1990.

_____. "Character Training for Youth." Late Works Vol. 9 of *The Complete Works of John Dewey 1882-1953*. Carbondale: Southern Illinois University Press, 1969-1990.

_____. *Education and the Social Order*. Late Works Vol. 9 of *The Complete Works of John Dewey 1882-1953*. Carbondale: Southern Illinois University Press, 1969-1990.

_____. *New York and the Seabury Investigation*. Late Works Vol. 9 of *The Complete Works of John Dewey 1882-1953*. Carbondale: Southern Illinois University Press, 1969-1990.

_____. *Logic: The Theory of Inquiry*. Late Works Vol. 12 of *The Complete Works of John Dewey 1882-1953*. Carbondale: Southern Illinois University Press, 1969-1990.

_____. *Experience and Education*. Late Works Vol. 13 of *The Complete Works of John Dewey 1882-1953*. Carbondale: Southern Illinois University Press, 1969-1990.

_____. "Does Human Nature Change?" Late Works Vol. 13 of *The Complete Works of John Dewey 1882-1953*. Carbondale: Southern Illinois University Press, 1969-1990.

_____ . "Theory of Valuation." Late Works Vol. 13 of *The Complete Works of John Dewey 1882-1953*. Carbondale: Southern Illinois University Press, 1969-1990.

_____ . "Liberating the Social Scientist." Late Works Vol. 15 of of *The Complete Works of John Dewey 1882-1953*. Carbondale: Southern Illinois University Press, 1969-1990.

II. GENERAL BIBLIOGRAPHY

Alderman, H. "Alasdair MacIntyre." Vol. 2 of *Encyclopedia of Ethics*. Edited by L. Becker. New York: Garland Publishing, 1992.

Aristotle. *The Politics of Aristotle*. Edited by W. L. Newman. Salem: Ayer Publishing, 1985.

_____ . *The Nichomachean Ethics*. Edited by W. L. Newman. Salem: Ayer Publishing, 1985.

Bellah, R. N., et al. *Habits of the Herat: Individualism and Commitment in American Life*. New York: Harper & Row, 1985.

Borradori, G. "Nietzsche or Aristotle?" *The American Philosopher*. Chicago: University of Chicago Press, 1994.

Brezinski, W. *Beliefs, Morals and Education*. Brookfield: Ashgate, 1994.

Burns, J. *Principles, Origins, and Establishment of the Catholic School System*. New York: Arno Press and the New York Times, 1969.

Coleman, James. *The Adolescent Society*. New York: The Free Press, 1961.

Cremin, Lawrence. *American Education: The Colonial Experience 1607-1783*. New York: Harper & Row, 1970.

_____ . *American Education: The National Experience 1783-1876*. New York: Harper & Row, 1980.

_____ . *American Education: The Metropolitan Experience 1876-1980*. New York: Harper & Row, 1988.

Damon, William. *Greater Expectations: Overcoming the Culture of Indulgence In America's Homes and Schools*. New York: The Free Press, 1995.

DeLattre, E. J. and W. E. Russell. "Schooling, Moral Principles, and the Formation of Character." *Boston University Journal of Education* 75, no. 2 (1993): 22-43.

Gardner, Howard. *The Unschooled Mind*. New York: Basic Books, 1992.

Gilligan, Carol. *In a Different Voice: Psychological Theory and Women's Development*. Cambridge: Harvard University Press, 1993.

Glendon, Mary Ann and David Blankenhorn, eds. *Seedbeds of Virtue*. New York: Madison Books, 1995.

Glickman, C.D. "The Essence of School Renewal: The Prose Has Begun." *Educational Leadership* 50, no. 1 (September 1992): 24-7.

Gordillo, M. V. *Desarrollo moral y educación*. Pamplona: Eunsa, 1992.

Hall, S. R. *Lectures on School-Keeping*. New York: Arno Press and the New York Times, 1969.

Hartshorne, H. and M.A. May. *Studies in the Nature of Character*. 3 vols. New York: MacMillan, 1928-1930.

Isaacs, David. *Teoría y práctica de la dirección de los centros educativos*. Paplona, Spain: Eunsa, 1995.

Kilpatrick, William. *Why Johnny Can't Tell Right from Wrong and What We Can Do About It*. New York: Simon & Schuster, 1992.

Kohlberg, Lawrence. *The Philosophy of Moral Development, Moral Stages and the Ideal of Justice*. San Francisco: Harper & Row, 1981.

Lapsley, D. K. "Pluralism, Virtues, and the Post-Kohlbergian Era in Moral Psychology." pp. 169-99 in *The Challenge of Pluralism*, edited by F. C. Power and D. K. Lapsley. South Bend: University of Notre Dame Press, 1992.

Lee, V. E. and H. M. Marks. "Sustained Effects of the Single-Sex Secondary School Experience on Attitudes, Behaviors and Values in College." in *Journal of Educational Psychology* 82, no. 3 (1990): 578-92.

Lickona, Thomas. *Educating for Character: How Our Schools Can Teach Respect and Responsibility*. New York: Bantam Books, 1991.

Lickona, Thomas. *Raising Good Children*. New York: Bantam Books, 1994.

Llano, Alejandro. "Presentación." pp. 11-17 in *Tres versiones rivales de la ética*. Madrid: Rialp, 1992.

MacIntyre, Alasdair. *After Virtue*. South Bend: University of Notre Dame Press, 1981.

_____ . *Three Rival Versions of Moral Inquiry*. South Bend: University of Notre Dame Press, 1990.

_____ . "The Privatization of Good: An Inaugural Lecture." *The Political Review* LII (1990): 344-61.

_____ . "Después de *Tras la virtud*: Una entrevista con Alasdair MacIntyre." By R. Yepes Stork. *Atlántida* 1 (1990): 453-61.

_____ . *How To Seem Virtuous Without Actually Being So*. Paper presented at the Centre for the Study of Cultural Values, Lancaster University, Lancaster, 1991.

_____ . "A Partial Response to My Critics." Pp. 283-304 in *After MacIntyre*, edited by J. Horton and S. Mendus. Cambridge: Polity Press, 1994.

McClellen, B.E. *Schools and the Shaping of Character*. Indiana University, Bloomington: Educational Research Information Center, 1992.

McKay, Roberta. "Character Education: A Question of Character." *Canadian Journal of Social Science* 28, no. 2 (Winter 1994): 46-7.

Millan Puelles, A. *La formación de la personalidad humana*. Madrid: Rialp, 1989.

Moore, C. "Restructured School: How, Why Do They Work?" *National Association of Secondary School Principals' Bulletin* 77, no. 553 (1993): 64-9.

Naval, Concepción. *Educar ciudadanos*. Pamplona: Eunsa, 1995.

Popenoe, D. "The Roots of Declining Social Virtue." pp. 71-104 in *Seedbeds of Virtue*, edited by M. A. Glendon and D. Blankenhorn. New York: Madison Books, 1995.

Power, F. C. "Moral Education and Pluralism." pp. 1-14 in *The Challenge of Pluralism*, edited by F. C. Power and D. K. Lapsley. South Bend: University of Notre Dame Press, 1992.

Riordan, Cornelius. *Girls and Boys in School: Together or Separate?* New York: Teachers College, Columbia University, 1990.

Ruiz, C. *Tradición, Universidad, y Virtud: Filosofía de la educación superior en Alasdair MacIntyre*. Ph.D. diss., University of Navarra, 1995.

Sandin, R. *The Rehabilitation of Virtue: Foundations of Moral Education*. New York: Praeger, 1992.

Sherman, N. *The Fabric of Character*. Oxford: Clavendon Press, 1989.

Sommers, C. and F. Sommers. *Vice and Virtue in Everyday Life*. Chicago: Harcourt Brace Jovanovich Publishers, 1989.

Sommers, Christina Hoff and Sally Satel. *One Nation Under Therapy*. New York: St. Martin's Press, 2005.

Spender, D. and E. Sarah. *Learning to Lose: Sexism and Education*. London: The Women's Press, 1989.

Stumpf, S. *Philosophy: History and Problems*. New York: McGraw-Hill, 1994.

Sykes, C. J. *Dumbing Down Our Kids*. New York: St. Martin's Press, 1995.

Tidball, M. E. "Women's Colleges and Women Achievers Revisited." *Signs: Journal of Women in Culture and Society* 5, no. 3 (Spring 1980): 504-17.

Williams, Mary. "Actions Speak Louder Than Words." *Educational Leadership* 51, no. 3 (November 1993): 22-23.

Wynne, E. and R. Ryan. *Reclaiming Our Schools*. New York: Merrill, 1993.

Yepes Stork, Ricardo. *Fundamentos de la antropología: Un ideal de la excelencia humana*. Pamplona: Eunsa, 1996.

PART I
Philosophy and Character Education

1. Aristotle, "Politics," in *The Politics of Aristotle*, ed. W. L. Newman (Salem: Ayer Publishing, 1985), VIII, 1, 1337a.

2. Alasdaire MacIntyre, *After Virtue* (South Bend: University of Notre Dame Press, 1981), 50.

3. Samuel Stumpf, *Philosophy: History and Problems* (New York: McGraw-Hill, 1994), 702-8.

4. Concepción Naval, *Educar ciudadanos*, 347-49.

Chapter 1 Historical Background

1. Lawrence Cremin, *American Education: The Colonial Experience, 1607-1783* (New York: Harper & Row, 1970), 22.

2. Adolfe Meyer, *An Educational History of the Western World* (New York: McGraw-Hill Book Company, 1965), 184.

3. B. Edward McClellen, *Schools and the Shaping of Character* (Bloomington: ERIC Clearing House for Social Studies/Social Science Education, 1992), 4-5.

4. Adolfe Meyer, *An Educational History*, 209-10.

5. Samuel Hall, *Lectures on School-Keeping* (New York: Arno Press and The New York Times, 1969), iv.

6. James A. Burns, *The Principles, Origin, and Establishment of the Catholic School System in the United States* (New York: Arno Press and The New York Times, 1969), 364.

7. Edward Wynne and Kevin Ryan, *Reclaiming Our Schools* (New York: Macmillan Publishing Company), 53.

Chapter 2 Current Trends

1. Robert Sandin, *The Rehabilitation of Virtue, Foundations of Moral education* (New York: Praeger, 1992), 56.

2. Charles Sykes, *Dumbing Down Our Kids* (New York: St. Martin's Press, 1995), 161.

3. Maria Victoria Gordillo, *Desarrollo moral y educación* (Pamplona, Spain: Eunsa, 1992), 92.

4. Lawrence Kohlberg, *The Philosophy of Moral Development, Moral Stages, and the Idea of Justice* (San Francisco: Harper & Row Publishers, 1981), 16.

5. Lawrence Kohlberg, "Moral Education Reappraised," *The Humanist*, vol. 38 (1978), 14.

6. Thomas Lickona, *Educating for Character* (New York: Bantam Books, 1991), 241.

7. William Damon, *Greater Expectations: Overcoming the Culture of Indulgence in America's Homes and Schools* (New York: The Free Press, 1995), 7-13.

8. Edwin J. DeLattre and William E. Russell, "Schooling, Moral Principles, and the Formation of Character," *Boston University Journal of Education*, vol. 175, no. 2 (1993): 38.

9. Christina Hoff Sommers and Sally Satel: *One Nation Under Therapy* (New York: St. Martin's Press, 2005), 11 – 53.

10.   Edwin J. DeLattre and William E. Russell, "Schooling, Moral Principles, and the Formation of Character," *Boston University Journal of Education*, vol. 175, no. 2 (1993): 36.

11.   Carol Gilligan, *In A Different Voice, Psychological Theory and Women's Development* (Cambridge, MA: Harvard Press, 1982).

12.   Maria Victoria Gordillo, *Desarrollo moral y educación* (Pamplona, Spain: Eunsa, 1992), 115.

PART II
John Dewey

Dewey the Man

1.   George Dykhuzien, *The Life and Mind of John Dewey* (Carbondale: Feffer & Simons, 1973), 1.

2.   John Dewey, "The Place of Religious Emotion" in *Early Works* (1886), 1:91.

3.   Lawrence Cremin, *American Education: The Metropolitan Experience, 1876-1890* (New York: Harper & Row Publishers, 1988), 168.

Chapter 1: Human Nature

1.   James Campbell, *Understanding John Dewey*, 38.

2.   John Dewey, "Individualism, Old and New" in *Later Works* (1930), vol. 5, 80-81.

3.   John Dewey, "Ethics" in *Middle Works* (1908), vol. 5, 388.

4.   John Dewey, "Reconstruction in Philosophy" in *Middle Works* (1920), vol. 12, 191.

5.   John Dewey, "The School and Society" in *Middle Works* (1899), vol. 1, 69.

6.   John Dewey, "Democracy and Education" in *Middle Works* (1916), vol. 9, 21.

7.   John Dewey, "Human Nature and Conduct" in *Middle Works* (1922), vol. 14, 77.

8.   John Dewey, "Freedom and Culture" in *Late Works* (1939), vol. 13, 77.

9.   John Dewey, "Psychology and Work" in *Late Works* (1930), vol. 5, 239.

10.   John Dewey, "Human Nature" in *Middle Works* (1922), vol. 14, 16.

11.   John Dewey, "Logic: The Theory of Inquiry" in *Late Works* (1903), vol. 12, 34.

12.   W. A. R. Leys, "Dewey's Social, Political, and Legal Philosophy" in *Guide to the Works of John Dewey*, 143-145.

13.   John Dewey, "Studies in Logical Theory" in *Middle Works* (1903), vol. 2, 307.

14.   John Dewey, "How We Think: A Restatement of the Relation of Reflective Thinking to the Educative Process" in *Late Works* (1933), vol. 8, 200.

15.   John Dewey, "Logic: The Theory of Inquiry" in *Late Works* (1903), vol. 12, 105-122.

Chapter 2: Morality & Growth

1.   John Dewey, "Ethics" in *Middle Works* (1908), vol. 5, 7.

2.   James Campbell, *Understanding John Dewey*, 110.

3.   John Dewey, "Human Nature and Conduct" in *Middle Works* (1922), vol. 14, 217

4.   John Dewey, "My Pedagogic Creed" in *Early Works* (1897), vol. 5, 64.

5.   John Dewey, "Ethics" in *Late Works* (1932), vol. 7, 176.
6.   John Dewey, "Moral Principles in Education" in *Middle Works* (1942), vol. 4, 277.
7.   John Dewey, "Ethics" in *Late Works* (1932), vol. 7, 315.
8.   John Dewey, "Liberating the Social Scientist" in *Late Works* (1947), vol. 15, 232-233.
9.   John Dewey, "Art as Experience" in *Late Works* (1934), vol. 10, 347.
10. James Campbell, *Understanding John Dewey*, 116.
11. John Dewey, "The Quest for Certainty: A Study of the Relation of Knowledge and Action" in *Late Works* (1929), vol. 4, 222.
12. John Dewey, "The Quest for Certainty": in *Late Works* (1929), vol. 4, 217.
13. John Dewey, "Theory of Valuation" in *Late Works* (1939), vol. 13, 229.
14. John Dewey, "Human Nature" in *Middle Works* (1922), vol. 14, 28.
15. John Dewey, "What I Believe" in *Late Works* (1930), vol. 5, 275.
16. John Dewey, "Reconstruction in Philosophy" in *Middle Works* (1920), vol. 12, 180-181.
17. John Dewey, "Self-Realization as the Moral Ideal" in *Early Works* (1893), vol. 4, 43.
18. John Dewey, "Reconstruction" in *Middle Works* (1920), vol. 12, 185.
19. John Dewey, "Experience and Education" in *Late Works* (1938), vol. 13, 19-24.
20. John Dewey, "Experience and Nature" in *Late Works* (1925), vol. 1, 57.
21. John Dewey, "Human Nature" in *Middle Works* (1922), vol. 14, 230.
22. John Dewey, "Does Human Nature Change?" in *Late Works* (1938), vol. 13, 286.
23. John Dewey, "The Quest for Certainty: A Study of the Relation of Knowledge and Action" in *Late Works* (1929), vol. 4, 209.
24. James Campbell, *Understanding John Dewey*, 140.

Chapter 3: Growth & Education

1.   John Dewey, "Democracy and Education" in *Middle Works* (1916), vol. 9, 46.
2.   John Dewey, "Education and Social Direction" in *Middle Works* (1918), vol. 11, 57.
3.   John Dewey, "Education as Politics" in *Middle Works* (1922), vol. 13, 334.
4.   John Dewey, "Ethics" in *Late Works* (1932), vol. 7, 364.
5.   James Campbell, *Understanding John Dewey*, 44.
6.   John Dewey, "The School and Society" in *Middle Works* (1899), vol. 1, 11.
7.   John Dewey, "Education" in *Late Works* (1934), vol. 9, 182.
8.   John Dewey, "Philosophy and Education" in *Late Works* (1930), vol. 5, 297.
9.   John Dewey, "New York and the Seabury Investigation" in *Late Works* (1933), vol. 9, 368-369.
10. John Dewey, "Social Purposes of Education" in *Middle Works* (1922), vol. 15, 161.
11. Cfr., John Dewey, "Democracy and Education in the World of Today" in *Late Works* (1938), vol. 13, 294-302.
12. John Dewey, "Education and the Social Order" in *Late Works* (1934), vol. 9, 180.
13. John Dewey, "Democracy and Educational Administration" in *Late Works* (1937), vol. 11, 222.
14. John Dewey, "My Pedagogic Creed" in *Early Works* (1897), vol. 5, 86, 84.
15. John Dewey, "The School and Society" in *Middle Works* (1899), vol. 1, 81.

Chapter 4: Character Training

1.   John Dewey, "Character Training for Youth" in *Late Works* (1934), vol. 9, 186.
2.   John Dewey, "The Need of an Industrial Education in an Industrial Society" in *Middle Works* (1916), vol. 10, 139.
3.   John Dewey, "Democracy and Education" in *Middle Works* (1916), vol. 9, 368.
4.   John Dewey, "Moral Principles in Education" in *Middle Works* (1942), vol. 4, 269.

PART III
Alasdair MacIntyre

1.   Giovanna Borradori, *The American Philosopher* (Chicago: University of Chicago Press, 1994), 140.
2.   Ricardo Yepes Stork, "Después de Tras la virtud: una entrevista con Alasdair MacIntyre," in *Atlántida*, (January, 1990), 453.
3.   H. Alderman, "Alasdair MacIntyre," in *Encyclopedia of Ethics,* ed. L. Becker (New York: Garland Publishing, Inc., 1992), 759.
4.   Alasdair MacIntyre, *After Virtue* (South Bend: University of Notre Dame Press, 1981), vii.
5.   H. Alderman, "Alasdair MacIntyre", 759.
6.   Alejandro Llano, "Presentación," *Tres versiones rivales de la ética* (Madrid: Rialp, 1992), 15.

Chapter 1: MacIntyre's Intellectual Framework

1.   Ricardo Yepes Stork, "Después de Tras la virtud", 454.
2.   Giovanna Borradori, *The American Philosopher*, 143.
3.   William Kilpatrick, *Why Johnny Can't Tell Right From Wrong and What We Can Do About It* (New York: Simon & Schuster, 1992), 14 – 29.
4.   Aristotle, "Nicomachean Ethics" in *The Politics of Aristotle*, ed. W. L. Newman (Salem: Ayer Publishing), I, 1, 1094a, 1-5.
5.   Aristotle, "Nicomachean Ethics", VI, 13, 1139a18.
6.   Aristotle, "Nicomachean Ethics", I, 13, 1103a15 – II, 1, 1103b26.
7.   Nancy Sherman, *The Fabric of Character* (Oxford: Clarendon Press, 1989), 2.
8.   Aristotle, "Nicomachean Ethics", I, 7, 109761.
9.   Aristotle, "Nicomachean Ethics", I, 1, 1095a20.
10. Aristotle, "Nicomachean Ethics", I, 1, 1099a30.
11. Aristotle, "Politics", in *The Politics of Aristotle*, ed. W. L. Newman (Salem: Ayer Publishing, 1985), I, 2, 1253a 3-4.
12. Aristotle, "Nicomachean Ethics", VIII, 1, 144b30 – 2
13. Alasdair MacIntyre, *After Virtue*, 190.
14. Alasdair MacIntyre, "A Partial Response to My Critics," in *After MacIntyre,* ed. J. Horton and S. Mendus (Cambridge: Polity Press, 1994), 284.
15. Aristotle, "Politics", I, 2, 1253a3-4.

Chapter 2: Practices and Traditions

1.   Alasdair MacIntyre, "A Partial Response", 284.
2.   Alasdair MacIntyre, *After Virtue*, 177
3.   Robert Bellah, *Habits of the Heart*, 153.

4.   Ricardo Yepes Stork, "Después de Tras la virtud", 461.
5.   Alasdair MacIntyre, "The Privatization of Good: An Inaugural Lecture", *The Review of Politics* LII (1990), 335.
6.   Ricardo Yepes Stork, "Después de Tras la virtud", 458.

Chapter 3: Educating for Good Character

1.   Claudia Ruiz, "Tradición y virtud: filosofía de la educación superior en Alasdair MacIntyre", (Ph.D. diss., Universidad de Navarra, Pamplona, Span, 1995), 626.
2.   Alasdair MacIntyre, "How to Seem Virtuous without Really Being So", (paper presented at the Centre for the Study of Cultural Values, Lancaster, England, 1991), 8.

PART IV
Person, Education & Society

1.   John Dewey, "The School and Society" in *Middle Works* (1899), vol. 1, 81.
2.   John Dewey, "Education and the Social Order" in *Late Works* (1934), vol. 9, 182.
3.   Roberta McKay, "Character Education: a Question of Character," *Canadian Social Studies*, vol. 28, no. 2 (winter, 1994): 46.
4.   William Kilpatrick, *Why Johnny Can't Tell Right from Wrong* (New York: Simon & Schuster, 1992), 25.
5.   "For virtue based theorists, the object of [character] education is to produce a virtuous individual. They therefore have much to say about education and character development. By concentrating attention on character rather than action, the philosopher of virtue tacitly assumes that a virtuous person's actions generally fall within the range of what is right and fair". Christina Sommers, *Vice and Virtue in Everyday Life* (Chicago, Harcourt Brace Jovnaovich Publishers, 1989): 2.
6.   Robert Sandin, *The Rehabilitation of Virtue*, 158-9.

Chapter 1: Philosophy & Mission Statements

1.   Wolfgang Brezinska, *Belief, Morals, and Education*, Brookfield: Ashgate, 1994, 1.
2.   David Isaacs, *Teoría y práctica de la dirección de los centros educativos*, Pamplona, Spain EUNSA, 1995, Chapter 4.
3.   The Willows Academy Brochure
4.   The Willows Academy, "Mission Statement, 2005, <http://www.willows.org/about.htm > (2 May 2005)
5.   <http://meriden.K12.ct.us/franklin/Franklin-WEB/about> (2 May, 2005)
6.   The PARED Foundation, <http://www.pared.edu.au/educationalprinciples.html> (2 May, 2005)
7.   <http://meriden.K12.ct.us/franklin/Franklin-WEB/about> (May 2, 2005)
8.   <http://www.phila.k12.pa.us/charter_schools/mission.html#> (2 May, 2005)
9.   < http://montroseschool.org/about_us.html> (May 2, 2005)
10. <http://www.phila.k12.pa.us/charter_schools/mission.html#> (May 2, 2005)
11. <http://www.phila.k12.pa.us/charter_schools/mission.html#> (2 May, 2005)

12. <http://www.emberselementary.org/mission.htm> (May 2, 2005)
13.<http://www.phila.k12.pa.us/charter_schools/mission.html#>
    (2 May, 2005)
14.<http:\\www.meriden.K12.ct.us/Lincoln/Lincoln_WEB/about/hotSchool.htm#mi
ssion> (2 May, 2005)

Chapter 2: Respect and Love of Learning

1. Edward Wynne and Kevin Ryan, *Reclaiming Our Schools*, 135-6.
2. Edwin Delattre, "Schooling, Moral Principles, and the Formation of Character," *Boston University Journal of Education*, vol. 75, n.2 (1993): 40.
3. William Kilpatrick, *Why Johnny Can't Tell Right From Wrong*, 26.
4. John Dewey, *Experience and Education*, 48.

Chapter 3: Character Education: Single-Sex or Coeducational?

1. Diane Rothenberg, "Supporting Girls in Early Adolescence," *ERIC Digest* (Urbana, ERIC Clearinghouse on Elementary and Early Childhood Education, 1995): 3.
2. V.E. Lee and H. M. Marks, "Sustained Effects of the Single-Sex Secondary School Experience on Attitudes, Behaviors, and Values in College," *Journal of Educational Psychology*, vol. 82, n. 3 (1990): 584.
3. Mary Ellen Tidball, "Women's Colleges and Women Achievers Revisited," *Signs: Journal of Women in Culture and Society*, (1980): 508.
4. Diane Rothenberg, "Supporting Girls in Early Adolescence," 2.
5. M. I. Rubenfeld and D. Gilroy, "Relationship between College Women's Occupational Interests and a Single-Sex Environment," *The Career Development Quarterly*, vol. 40, (1991) 64.
6. Cornelius Riordan, *Girls and Boys in School: Together or Separate?* (New York, Teachers College, Columbia University 1990): 61.
7. Diane Spender and Elizabeth Sarah, *Learning, to Lose, Sexism and Education*, (London, The Women's Press, 1989): 87.
8. Joy K. Rice, "Separation and the Education of Women," *Initiatives*, vol. 53, n. 3 (Fall 1991): 9.
9. James Coleman, *The Adolescent Society*, (New York: The Free Press, 1961): 50-1.
10. M. I. Rubenfeld and D. Gilroy, "Relationship between College Women's Occupational Interests and a Single-Sex Environment," *The Career Development Quarterly*, vol. 40, (1991) 64.
11. Diane Spender and Elizabeth Sarah, *Learning, to Lose*, 89.
12. John Goodlad concluded in 1984 "junior and senior high school youth are excessively preoccupied with physical appearance and popularity in the peer group, games, and athletics." *A Place Called School*, (New York: MacGraw-Hill. 1984): 75. (A rapid survey of the prevailing subculture in high school in the early twentieth century would undoubtedly yield the same results.)
13. Jennifer Shaw, "Education and Individual Schooling for Girls or Mixed Schools – A Mixed Blessing?" in *Schooling for Women's Work*, ed. R. Deem (London: Routledge & Kegan Paul, 1976): 137.
14. Diane Spender and Elizabeth Sarah, *Learning, to Lose*, 88, 89.

Chapter 4: Creating a Tradition of Virtue

1.   Charles E. Moore, "Restructured Schools: How, Why do They Work?" in *NAASP Bulletin*, vol. 77, n. 553 (1993): 64.

2.   Carl D. Glickman, "The Essence of School Renewal: The Prose Has Begun," in *Educational Leadership*, vol. 50, n. 1 (September, 1992): 24.

3.   Mary M. Williams, "Actions Speak Louder Than Words: What Students Think," in *Educational Leadership*, vol. 51, n. 3 (1993): 22.

4.   Mary Williams, "Actions Speak Louder Than Words," 22.

5.   Ibid. 23.

Chapter 5: School & Family:
Creating a Community of Shared Interests

1.   Ricardo Yepes Stork,"Después de Tras la virtud," 92.

2.   F. Clark Power, "Moral Education and Pluralism," in *The Challenge of Pluralism*. ed. F. Clark Power and D. K. Lapsley (South Bend: Notre Dame Press, 1992) 2.

3.   David Popenoe, "The Roots of Declining Social Virtue," *Seedbeds of Virtue*, 86-7.

4.   Daniel K. Lapsley, "Pluralism, Virtues, and the Post-Kohlbergian Era in Moral Psychology," *The Challenge of Pluralism*, 195.

5.   Wolfgang Brezinski, *Beliefs, Morals, and Education* (Brookfield: Ashgate, 1994), 139.

6.   Edwin J. DeLattre and William E. Russell, "Schooling, Moral Principles, and the Formation of Character," *Boston University Journal of Education*, vol. 175, no. 2 (1993): 38, 39.

7.   David Rosenthal and Julanne Sawyers, "Building Successful Home/School Partnerships, Strategies for Parent Support and Involvement," *Childhood Education*, Summer (1996): 194

8.   Edwin J. DeLattre and William E. Russell, "Schooling, Moral Principles, and the Formation of Character," *Boston University Journal of Education*, vol. 175, no. 2 (1993): 36

9.   William Kilpatrick, *Why Johnny Can't Tell Right From Wrong and What We Can Do About It* (New York: Simon & Schuster 1992), 254-5.

10.   Thomas Lickona, *Raising Good Children* (New York: Bantam Books 1994) 329.

11.   Thomas Lickona, *Raising Good Children* (New York: Bantam Books 1994) 330.

About the Author

Holly Salls lives in Chicago, where she has taught at The Willows Academy for twenty-five years. Her experiences range from teaching French, Spanish, Old Testament, and Classical Philosophy to Virtue Through Literature courses. She has also served as Assistant Head of School and as Director of Character Education, at which time she created a character education program based on some of the ideas found in this book. Ms. Salls received her B.A. from The University of Wisconsin, Madison and her M.A. from The University of Navarre, Pamplona, Spain.

Ms. Salls is active in promoting character education among parents, serving for six years as the editor of the monthly newsletter, "Tidbits for Parents". She has also produced character education articles for High School students entitled "Tidbits for Teens."

In addition to her work at The Willows Academy, Ms. Salls currently writes English and Spanish parent newsletters in association with Link Institute. These newsletters offer concrete suggestions for implementing Link Institute's *Core Virtues Program* in the home.